Long Drums and Canons

Teaching and Researching African Literatures

Bernth Lindfors

Africa World Press, Inc.
P. O. Box 1892
Trenton, NJ 08607

Copyright © 1995, Bernth Lindfors

First Printing, 1995

Cover Design by Linda Nickens

Library of Congress Cataloging-in-Publication Data:

Lindfors, Bernth.
     Long drums and canons : teaching and researching African
literatures / Bernth Lindfors.
       p.   cm
    Includes bibliographical references (p.   ) and index.
     ISBN 0-86543-436-0. -- ISBN 0-86543-437-9 (pbk.)
      1. African literature--Study and teaching.   2. African literature
(English)--Study and teaching.   3. African literature--Study and
teaching--United States. I. Title.
PL8009.8.L56   1995
896'.007--dc20   94-37182
                                                 CIP

Table of Contents

Table of Contents, continued

Acknowledgements

I am grateful to the journal editors of *Commonwealth: Essays and Studies; Council on National Literatures Report; Matatu; Modern Language Association Newsletter; Nsukka Studies in African Literature;* and *Wasafiri;* and to the book editors of *Teaching English in African Schools: Four Lectures; The Teaching of African Literature; African Literature Studies: The Present State/L'État Present; Autobiographical and Biographical Writing in the Commonwealth; Critical Theory and African Literature; A Shaping of Connections: Commonwealth Literature Studies Then and Now;* and *South Asian Responses to Chinua Achebe* for permission to reprint material that first appeared in their pages.

I also wish to express my gratitude to the University Research Institute at The University of Texas at Austin for providing funds for typesetting this book, to my daughter Susan for doing the initial typing, and to Cinde Hastings for preparing the final camera-ready copy.

Introduction

Teaching and researching African literatures are relatively new academic enterprises. Forty years ago hardly anyone was engaged in such activities, but today hundreds of teachers throughout the world are introducing thousands of students to the vigorous literatures that have emerged on the African continent. These educators are also writing numerous books and articles on what they teach, producing a voluminous literature on these literatures. Within a single generation they have transformed the study of African literatures into a young but respectable discipline, a distinct branch of scholarship with its own history, politics, rituals, and polemics. One could say without too much exaggeration that interpretation of African literatures has already become a recognized profession.

Africa itself has been the locus of most of this institutionalized activity. In schools and universities throughout the continent, literature curricula have been revamped to accommodate works by indigenous authors. Special libraries and research centers have been built, new journals founded, chairs and professorships of literature established, and national and regional scholarly bodies formed, all with the aim of promoting further research and teaching in this burgeoning field. African literature scholarship has become a major growth industry in the African academic world.

The same has happened elsewhere but at a slightly slower pace. African literatures were immediately accepted as legitimate subject matter in African, Black and ethnic studies programs at American universities, but they made their way more gradually into English, French, Portuguese, and comparative literature departments, where at first they tended to be regarded as exotic additions to a core syllabus consisting of classic Western texts. Today demands for a multicultural curriculum that is not totally dominated by books written by "dead white males" have led to the incorporation of more non-Western literature in required undergraduate courses, so one now sometimes finds African novels, plays or poems being read alongside American and European works. This kind of curricular innovation has occurred at the high school level too, especially in schools with a sizable minority enrollment. In this way texts that used to be at the outer periphery of literary studies in the United States have started to infiltrate the mainstream.

Teachers confronted with the challenge of teaching these new texts have turned to informed scholars and critics for guidance, so there has also been an ever-expanding market for books and articles on African masterworks. But part of the problem here has been to find a reliable way to identify the masterworks. Who are the most important African authors and which are their most significant writings? There has been considerable debate on such questions, and though not all of the dust stirred up by the debaters has settled yet, it could be said that a consensus of opinion can be discovered by examining which authors the critics choose to write about and which texts the teachers ultimately choose to teach. In other words, a canon does exist because those who are professionally engaged in interpreting African literatures do discriminate when selecting what to comment on. Writers who command attention are *ipso facto* more important than writers who are ignored. The biggest trees in any chosen forest are always clearly visible.

Having studied and taught African literatures for more than thirty years, I have frequently had occasion to address issues relating to pedagogical, disciplinary and canonical matters. Collected here are some of the contributions I have made to ongoing discussions of teaching and research. Although several of these interventions were made long ago, I have included them because they deal with problems that are still unresolved today, particularly in environments that have been slow to embrace curricular reform. The basic premise underlying all these essays is that African literatures are worthy of study not only in Africa itself but also in every other part of the world that values the stimulation and pleasure to be derived from reading excellent writing.

Austin, Texas
July 15, 1994

Opening Up the Canon

hy Not African Literature?*

Sounds of a Cowhide Drum

> Boom! Boom! Boom!
> I hear it far in the northern skies—
> a rumble and a roar as of thunder.
>
> I prick my ears
> like a buck ready to flee from an imminent storm.
>
> Boom! Boom! Boom!
> As it rolls nearer
> and nearer to the southern sky
> it holds my heart,
> my hopes soaring high into the eagle's throne.
>
> Boom! Boom! Boom!
> I am the drum on your dormant soul,
> cut from the black hide of a sacrificial cow.
>
> I am the spirit of your ancestors,
> habitant in hallowed huts,
> eager to protect,
> forever vigilant.
>
> Let me tell you of your precious heritage,
> of your glorious past trampled by the conqueror,
> destroyed by the zeal of a missionary.

* Lecture delivered at a conference of the English Academy of Southern Africa
  held in Roma, Lesotho, January 1973.

I lay bare facts for scrutiny
by your searching mind,
all declarations and dogmas.

O! Hear me, Child!
in the Zulu dance
shaking their hearts into a frenzy.

O! Hear me, Child!
in the night vigils of black Zionists
lifting their spirits into ecstasy.

Boom! Boom! Boom!
That is the sound of a cowhide drum —
the Voice of Mother Africa.

Oswald Mtshali (68)

It is about the Voice of Mother Africa that I wish to speak today. Too many people still believe Africa to be mute, inarticulate, tongue-tied by the hundreds of vernacular languages spoken between Cape Town and Timbuktu. Too many still cling to the opinion that Africa has contributed nothing of value to world literature, that she is incapable of mature self-expression in an international lingua franca such as English or French. Like Caliban, she may have been fortunate enough to learn Prospero's language but being a "savage...a thing most brutish" (Shakespeare 23), she learned it imperfectly and therefore has never been able to sing as sweetly as her colonial master. As Caliban once put it to Prospero, "You taught me language; and my profit on't/Is, I know how to curse" (24).

Since Prospero did not care to hear Caliban's curses, he failed to recognize their poetry, preferring to dismiss their alien and sometimes jarring rhythms as the "gabble" of an "abhorred slave" (23), as tangible evidence of a half-civilized creature's ill will. Prospero, apparently, was so preoccupied with the administration of his island kingdom that he never took time to listen attentively to the sounds of a cowhide drum. He never discovered the beauties of indigenous music.

The men and women who devise literature syllabuses for African secondary schools are the Prosperos of our day. Instead of making use of local literary resources to create something meaningful and relevant for Africa, they turn their eyes toward England, import ponderous verbal artifacts from that remote and dying culture, and try to set them up as monuments worthy of universal veneration. Some of these artifacts are genuine antiques from Elizabethan times; others are curios and shop-worn souvenirs that have no more validity in the latter third of the twentieth century than do horse-drawn carriages and gas-lit street lamps. And virtually all of them must be extensively explicated before they make any sense at all to the young African reader whose entire future may hang on his ability to crack the difficult, often archaic, linguistic code in which they are written. The student learns not to read but to decipher these strange foreign texts which begin to assume the importance of Holy Writ and are studied every bit as religiously. Prospero may think he is working magic by converting young Yorubas, Kikuyus, Zulus, and Boers into reasonable facsimiles of cultivated Englishmen, but he actually is wreaking havoc by destroying the capacity of educated Africans to read for enjoyment and respond intelligently to literary art. Moreover, he is implanting the pernicious notion that Africans have created no literature worthy of serious attention and that all the best writing in the English language has emanated from the British Isles. The result is a form of intellectual colonialism which accepts as its basic premise the idea that Africa still needs the civilizing influence of Europe. For such arrogant presumption and blind ethnocentrism, Prospero, despite his good intentions, deserves all of Caliban's curses.

Intellectual colonialism is a crippling affliction that invariably outlives political colonialism. Even after the Calibans of the world have risen up and thrown off Prospero's yoke, they continue to do things according to his laws and formulas, behaving as if he were still in command and looking over their shoulder. Those who suggest trying new approaches to old problems are looked upon with suspicion and distrust, if not outright dread, for they are advocates of the unfamiliar and unknown. No one is willing to risk making a fresh start and proceeding in a totally new direction for fear of "lowering the standards" set during the colonial era. Revolutionary energies quickly dissipate under the oppressive weight of lockstep conservatism and rigor mortis sets in, especially in educational institutions. Syllabuses stiffen into rigid petrification, preserving anachronistic educational objectives and outmoded pedagogical practices like the fossil bones of extinct dinosaurs. Thus the freest Africans frequently become the most intellectually enslaved.

If we wish to devise a literature curriculum which speaks directly to high school students in southern Africa in a modern idiom they can immediately understand and appreciate, a language that does not require the linguistic mediation of a teacher-translator, we must begin by discarding the musty heirlooms and bric-a-brac of the past. We must release the syllabus from the stranglehold of Shakespeare. We must shut out the poets who wrote in England more than a hundred years ago. We must put the longwinded Victorian novelists back into cold storage. We must do everything necessary, everything possible, to change the program of literature studies so that students emerge with a love for reading. This, after all, is the stated objective of the Joint Matriculation Board: "To encourage in the pupil a love of and interest in English literature so that he will read English books of his own accord." (One optimistically assumes that the word "English" is used here to mean the language rather than the nationality of the author.) One way to achieve this objective is to modernize the syllabus so that students read books written in relatively recent times about matters of contemporary concern. Another way is to Africanize the syllabus so that they read about peoples and places which are not completely outside the orbit of their own personal experience.

The best way would be to both modernize and Africanize the entire literature curriculum.

Before pursuing this argument further, it is necessary to pause a moment to document the absurdity of the present syllabus, at least as it is reflected in the lower grade English examinations of the Joint Matriculation Board from December 1969 to March 1972. I have not been able to examine the full curriculum for these years, so my remarks must be based on the questions set for the literature exams. The questions reveal that the following authors and works were studied intensively:

Drama: Shakespeare, *Julius Caesar* and *Richard III*
Fiction: George Eliot, *Adam Bede*
  Mark Twain, *Tom Sawyer*
  Thomas Hardy, *Under the Greenwood Tree*
Poetry: Herrick, "To Daffodils"
  Wordsworth, "I Wandered Lonely as a Cloud"
  Keats, "To Autumn," "On First Looking into
    Chapman's Homer"
  Auden, "Musée des Beaux Arts"

Notice that the only twentieth-century author on the list is Auden and his poem "Musée des Beaux Arts" requires considerable knowledge of European culture. To refresh your memory, here is the entire text:

About suffering they were never wrong,
The Old Masters: how well they understood
Its human position; how it takes place
While someone else is eating or opening a window or just walking
    dully along;
How, when the aged are reverently, passionately waiting
For the miraculous birth, there always must be
Children who did not specially want it to happen, skating
On a pond at the edge of the wood:
They never forgot

That even the dreadful martyrdom must run its course
Anyhow in a corner, some untidy spot
Where the dogs go on with their doggy life and the torturer's horse
Scratches its innocent behind on a tree.

In Brueghel's *Icarus*, for instance: how everything turns away
Quite leisurely from the disaster; the ploughman may
Have heard the splash, the forsaken cry,
But for him it was not an important failure; the sun shone
As it had to on the white legs disappearing into the green
Water; and the expensive delicate ship that must have seen
Something amazing, a boy falling out of the sky,
Had somewhere to get to and sailed calmly on. (Auden 146-47)

This poem would seem to meet all the requirements of modernity: the vocabulary is simple, the syntax uncomplicated, the diction conversational, the poetic effects subtle and unobtrusive, the message direct, the matter significant. It would seem an ideal poem for use in African secondary schools but for the blunt fact that it cannot be completely understood without a minimal knowledge of Flemish Renaissance painting, Greek mythology, and the contemplative habits of visitors to European art museums. The examiners would even go a step further and have the student learn a bit of French; the first thing they demand is "the name of the author and the title of the poem" (2 marks). But this question is innocent compared to those that follow: "What is Brueghel's 'Icarus'?" (2 marks); "How did the boy come to be in the sky, and what caused him to fall?" (6 marks); "Who were 'The Old Masters'?" (part of 6 marks). To answer these questions, the student must have crammed a number of cultural facts into his head which are necessary as background information to the poem but are totally foreign to his own cultural experience. Moreover, these facts are extrinsic to the poem itself; to learn them the student must go beyond the words on the page and seek explanations from his teacher, from an encyclopedia, or from an annotated textbook. He must become a research scholar bent on mastering every squiggle of the cryptic cipher. To him an English poem is not a song but an obscure riddle, every mystifying nuance of which must be laboriously interpreted and committed to memory.

I would not dwell on this point if such questions were the exception rather than the rule on English literature examinations. But it is clear, even from the small sample I have seen, that the examiners are often far more interested in what the student has been able to learn about the cultural ambiance out of which a particular English poem has emerged than they are in how capably the student responds to the art of poetry. For instance, in the same examination in which the questions about Auden's poem appear, we find the following questions about Keats's "On First Looking into Chapman's Homer": "Who is Homer?"; "Name the two works that constituted his demesne"; "To what work of Chapman's does this line refer?" One is almost surprised that the students have not been asked to identify stout Cortez or tell why Keats mistakenly placed him on that peak in Darien, but perhaps these questions have been saved for a later examination. One must not exhaust the arsenal of irrelevance in a single year.

The questions on Shakespeare pay closer attention to the text but only because the text demands it. Elizabethan English in all its florid glory is virtually a foreign language to the modern English teenager. How much more bewildering it must seem to the African student who has learned English as a second or third language. It is therefore not surprising that so many of the questions on *Julius Caesar* and *Richard III* ask, "What does this line mean?" or "Explain this statement in your own words." Simple comprehension is the crux of the problem for studying Shakespeare. Again, it is the slave who has been most rigorously drilled, the linguist who has been most thoroughly initiated into the mysterious cult of arcane rhetoric, the pedant who has memorized every footnote, who gets rewarded, who wins the examination sweepstakes. All interpretation continues to come directly from above. The student's job is merely to suck up what he can, filter it through his consciousness, and flush it out at the appropriate moment. No love for literature blossoms from this dreary process. Transforming oneself into an efficient intellectual water-closet is very hard work, especially when one has to wrestle with heavy, outdated materials, and no African who has been through such torture is likely to remember it as an experience he would voluntarily repeat later in his life. One wonders how many African graduates have read any Shakespeare that has not been required for an English examination. One wonders how many have joyfully returned to Herrick, Wordsworth, Keats, or Auden to work out the cultural conundrums that even their poetry sometimes presents to non-English readers. One wonders how many have had their interest in reading killed rather than kindled by the high school English literature syllabus. It may sound as if I am exaggerating the problem by singling out a few bad examination questions and condemning them as typical of the orientation of the entire syllabus. Improve the questions, some would say, and you will redeem the curriculum. A bandage here, some plaster there, and everything will be all right—the system is not as sick as it seems. But I am arguing that major surgery is needed if we are interested in saving the system from further deterioration and ultimate collapse. We must transplant the heart of the syllabus if we want to give it new life. We must change not only the examination questions but the books upon which they are based. There is bound to be some resistance to this idea from government officials, educational authorities, teachers, parents, even the students themselves. Old habits die hard, and major curricular innovations are usually very difficult to introduce. In this case the conservative academic spine is likely to be even stiffer than usual because the books I am recommending are African rather than English. One can anticipate at least five different kinds of arguments against Africanizing the literature syllabus—the qualitative, the linguistic, the cultural, the political, and the pedagogical. Let us examine these one by one.

1. *The qualitative argument.* Some will say that African literary works are not of the same high quality as the English works in the present syllabus, most of which have already passed the test of time and are widely regarded as classics of literature. To substitute an African play for *Richard III*, an African novel for *Adam Bede*, or an African poem for Herrick's "To Daffodils" would be to lower the literary standards of the examination and thereby deflate the value of a high school diploma. The African student would be given an education inferior to that of his peers in England.

2. *The linguistic argument.* Since most African authors have English as their second or third language, they cannot be expected to have achieved a mastery of it equal to that of the gifted native speaker. Their writing will reflect regional dialectal deviations from standard English as well as occasional grammatical errors. Students will no longer have a trustworthy model from which they can learn to speak and write proper English.

3. *The cultural argument.* If English classics are removed from the literature syllabus, African students will be deprived of the opportunity to read great books about a culture different from their own. They will lose all contact with the rich literary heritage of Western civilization and will find nothing of comparable value to replace it. They will no longer be liberally educated citizens of the wider world.

4. *The political argument.* Too many African literary works focus on contemporary political problems and such subject-matter is unacceptable at the secondary school level. Since the political history of Africa varies from region to region, many of these books will not be relevant to the experience of southern Africans. Moreover, some of them written by black and coloured South Africans have been banned in the Republic of South Africa.

5. *The pedagogical argument.* High school teaching materials on contemporary African literature are still quite scarce, especially in southern Africa, where such literature has never been used in schools before. Without adequate background information and helpful literary criticism on an assigned book, teachers and students would be lost. There is much more material available on English classics.

To these arguments we can offer the following counter-considerations.

Qualitative considerations
First, literary quality will not be sacrificed if the African texts are selected with more care and intelligence than have customarily been expended in selecting books for English literature examinations in southern Africa. The guiding principle of selection up till now appears to have been a mixture of old-fashioned trophy hunting and Anglo-Saxon ancestor worship; it was necessary each year to fish up something respectable from the standing pool of classic works by classic English authors. The rules were fairly simple: we must have a play—any play at all—by Shakespeare, we must have a solid Victorian novel, and we must have a poetry anthology rich in Romanticism, representative of the Renaissance, and light on the less predictable Moderns. The content, form, and style of these revered classics did not matter so much as the fact that they were indeed revered classics. Any amount of genial scatology would be permitted so long as it were perpetrated by Shakespeare. Any queer dialect would be condoned if it came from the pen of Dickens or Hardy. Any aberrant or obsolete English word or unusual syntactical structure would be tolerated in a poem by one of the certified immortals. After all, one of the stated aims of the English curriculum was "to extend the pupil's command of spoken and written English." What better way could this be done than to give the student a full dose of the literary genius of

the true creators of the English language? Pick a classic, almost any classic, and you will have chosen a winner on every score.

Every score, that is, but ready intelligibility. The English classics, especially the most antiquated pieces, are often far more difficult to understand than is generally admitted (except by students preparing for the matriculation exams). Both the language and the cultural bias of an English author may be bewildering to young Africans who have never previously encountered royal rhetoric, Homeric epics, Roman history, English social customs, or even a host of golden daffodils. These problems would disappear overnight if we could substitute the best modern African works for the tired British museum pieces. We would have to proceed cautiously and select wisely to ensure that one type of unintelligibility were not replaced by another, but I am confident that an entirely African syllabus could be devised that would be more meaningful and relevant to the experience of students in southern Africa and would teach them much more about language, literature, and life than the present syllabus could hope to do. And all this could be accomplished without sacrificing quality.

I am aware, of course, that intelligibility and relevance do not necessarily guarantee excellence in a work of literary art. The most pornographic potboiler could be said to be intelligible and relevant to a certain audience, but this alone would not make it great literature. A book's quality must be judged by other criteria as well—beauty of form, brilliance of language, felicity of characterization, aptness of dramatic action, high moral seriousness, etc. But even by these criteria I would insist that the best African literary works compare favorably with any of the titles currently on the literature syllabus and in many ways surpass them as verbal artifacts created out of images, metaphors, and symbols able to move the hearts and minds of living human beings. For the best African literary works are modern classics that distill the essence of significant contemporary experience into permanent artistic form.

The timid will ask, How can we be sure they are modern classics? How can we tell they will endure? If we accept the dictionary definition of a classic as a "literary work of the first rank and of acknowledged excellence," how can we be absolutely certain that they measure up to world standards of aesthetic discrimination? The answer to these questions is that some African literary works have already proven themselves classics. Some have withstood an abbreviated test of time and popularity by never going out of print since the day they were published fifteen or twenty years ago. Considering the mutability of contemporary literary fashions and the vagaries of bookselling in many parts of Africa, this in itself is quite an impressive achievement. But besides being best sellers, certain books have also won international literary prizes and worldwide acclaim as outstanding works of fiction, drama, or poetry. A few have even been adopted as required texts for high school matriculation examinations. A book like Chinua Achebe's *Things Fall Apart*, for instance, is currently compulsory reading in secondary schools in West Africa, East Africa, parts of India, and Australia. Seven and a half years ago the London *Times Literary Supplement* stated that "Already *Things Fall Apart* is probably as big a factor in the formation of a young West African's picture of his past, and of his relation to it, as any of the still rather distorted teachings of the pulpit and the primary school" (Anon. 79). If this novel is so important in other parts of Africa and so widely read elsewhere, why doesn't it appear on the English literature syllabus in southern Africa? Why is it not considered as worthy of textbook status as *Adam Bede, Tom Sawyer* or the relatively unknown *Under the Greenwood Tree*? It is clearly as much an African classic as the novels by Eliot and Hardy are European classics or as *Tom Sawyer* is an American classic. Furthermore, it is a book to which African students of any tribe or race will immediately respond, for it tells a story highly relevant to contemporary African experience in a language all can understand. It is likely to generate more discussion, more active thinking, more enthusiasm than any of the books selected by the

Joint Matriculation Board between 1969 and 1972. And in the process it will certainly instill a greater love for reading than has ever before been instilled in African students by "English classics." In West Africa *Things Fall Apart* has even been known to encourage young men and women to try writing fiction. In other words, it has taught many young people that literature is not a dull, recondite art that they must struggle to decode but a living art in which they themselves can creatively participate. It has literally helped resurrect literature from the realm of the dead. If this does not prove its artistic excellence and enduring value, I do not know what can. African classics need not be ancient to be truly great.

Linguistic considerations
The argument that African writers use substandard or irregular English is based on the erroneous assumption that no one can completely master a second language. It is believed that Africans write English as peculiarly as they speak it; that is, with some kind of unusual intonation or quirky accent that distinguishes it from the "normal" English used by the "average" native speaker, a mythical creature who enunciates every word crisply in a BBC baritone. Because Africans frequently depart from this "standard," says the conventional wisdom, their writings cannot be trusted as models of proper English usage.

The notion that all good Englishmen speak and write alike is of course absurd. There are probably more different dialects of English in use in the British Isles than there are in all the anglophonic areas of Africa put together. For a native speaker to complain about a non-native dialect when his own dialect may depart an equal distance from any arbitrary norm is for the pot to call the kettle black. Dialects will forever be with us and it is no doubt a good thing they will. They enrich rather than impoverish the English language.

The more pertinent issue as far as African literature is concerned is whether it is worthwhile for an African author to attempt to write in pristine Oxbridge English. If he does so, he discovers he must falsify the people and culture he is portraying in order to maker them fit an alien linguistic mould. What African villager, supposedly speaking in a vernacular language, would address his listeners in a Shavian or Churchillian idiom? What tribal palaver would be argued in the over-polite rhetoric of Westminster and Whitehall? The African author must either compromise reality or take liberties with his linguistic medium. Many talented African authors have done the latter, creating new prose styles in English that simulate idiomatic expression in a variety of indigenous African tongues. They have learned to translate the particularity of their cultural experience into a universal language without sacrificing the integrity of the experience or the intelligibility of the language. Chinua Achebe was speaking for all Africans writing in English when he said,

> My answer to the question: *Can an African ever learn English well enough to be able to use it effectively in creative writing?* is certainly yes. If on the other hand you ask: *Can he ever learn to use it like a native speaker?* I should say, I hope not. It is neither necessary nor desirable for him to be able to do so. The price a world language must be prepared to pay is submission to many different kinds of use. The African writer should aim to use English in a way that brings out his message best without altering the language to the extent that its value as a medium of international exchange will be lost. He should aim at fashioning out an English which is at once universal and able to carry his peculiar experience....I feel that the English language will be able to carry the weight of my African experience. But it will have to be a new English, still in full communion with its ancestral home but altered to suit its new African surroundings. (*Morning* 62-63)

The African writer must actively seek to create this new English. He must be the master, not slave, of his adopted tongue.

But the schoolmarm's question will still be asked: Can deliberate stylistic innovations, conscious departures from standard usage, serve as practical models for students who are trying to learn to speak and write better English? The answer is, it all depends on how radical the innovations are, how daring the departures from modern convention happen to be. If the style is as baroque as Shakespeare's, as latinate as Milton's, or as plethoric as Dickens's at his windiest, then I think no useful purpose will be served by studying it. In language learning, one quickly reaches a point of diminishing returns with authors whose every utterance requires dictionary detective work. Literature study should not be a boring exercise in semantic explication. But if an author succeeds in creating a new style which is not obscure and which takes full advantage of hitherto unexploited resources of the English language to convey an important message, then I think students can profit from exposure to it. What I have in mind is the conscious artistry of skilled literary craftsmen such as Chinua Achebe, Gabriel Okara, and Wole Soyinka—writers who bend the English language to their own purposes without breaking it. To put it in Achebe's words, each fashions out "an English which is at once universal and able to carry his peculiar experience."

Let us look at a few examples. One of the most frequently quoted excerpts from Achebe's novels is a passage from *Arrow of God* in which an Ibo chief priest explains to his son why he is intending to send him to a mission school. In imagery appropriate to the culture in which the story is set, Achebe has the priest say:

> I want one of my sons to join these people and be my eye there. If there is nothing in it you will come back. But if there is something there you will bring home my share. The world is like a Mask dancing. If you want to see it well you do not stand in one place. My spirit tells me that those who do not befriend the white man today will be saying *had we known* tomorrow. (55)

Notice that every image, every comparison, every proverb, literally every *word* in this passage is firmly rooted in the culture Achebe portrays. The style is not "normal" English because it represents the way an Ibo would express himself in his own language. Achebe is well aware of the crucial difference this fact makes. In an article on "The English Language and the African Writer," he once demonstrated that he could have written this passage in a totally different style, a more orthodox English prose:

> I am sending you as my representative among these people—just to be on the safe side in case the new religion develops. One has to move with the times or else one is left behind. I have a hunch that those who fail to come to terms with the white man may well regret their lack of foresight. (*Morning* 62)

Obviously this is the King's English rather than the chief priest's Ibo. Achebe points out "The material is the same. But the form of the one is *in character* and the other is not. It is largely a matter of instinct, but judgment comes into it too" (62). Achebe is one of a new breed of African writers who exercise instinct and judgment to express African ideas in the English language.

Gabriel Okara is another, and his bold experiments in style in a novel called *The Voice* surpass Achebe's in scope and imagination. His ambition is "to keep as close as possible to the vernacular expressions. For, from a word, a group of words, a sentence and even a name in any African language, one can glean the social norms, attitudes and values of a people" (*Transition* 15). Okara tries to reproduce even the reduplicated words, multiple adjective compounds, and syntactical structures of his mother tongue in English. The result might have been a disaster in the hands of a less disciplined artist, but Okara, a skilled poet, knows how to control sound, rhythm, image, and design to create striking lyrical effects. Here is how *The Voice* opens:

> Some of the townsmen said Okolo's eyes were not right, his head was not correct. This they said was the result of his knowing too much book, walking too much in the bush, and others said it was due to his staying too long alone by the river.
> So the town of Amatu talked and whispered; so the world talked and whispered. Okolo had no chest, they said. His chest

was not strong and he had not shadow. Everything in this world that spoiled a man's name they said of him, all because he dared to search for *it*. He was in search of *it* with all his inside and with all his shadow.

Okolo started his search when he came out of school and returned home to his people. When he returned home to his people, words of the coming thing, rumours of the coming thing, were in the air flying like birds, swimming like fishes in the river. But Okolo did not join them in their joy because what was there was no longer there and things had no more roots. So he started his search for *it*. And this stopped the Elders from slapping their thighs in joy because of the coming thing. (9-10)

Now here is another passage showing some of the syntactical irregularities to be found in *The Voice*:

It was the day's ending and Okolo by a window stood. Okolo stood looking at the sun behind the tree tops falling. The river was flowing, reflecting the finishing sun, like a dying away memory. It was like an idol's face, no one knowing what is behind. Okolo at the palm trees looked. They were like women with their hair hanging down, dancing, possessed. Egrets, like white flower petals strung slackly across the river, swaying up and down, were returning home. And, on the river, canoes were crawling home with bent backs and tired hands, paddling. A girl with only a cloth tied around her waist and the half-ripe mango breasts, paddled, driving her paddle into the river with a sweet inside. (13)

I can still hear the uneasy questions. Is this really English prose? Is it prudent to set Okara up as a model for young Africans to emulate? Do we actually want our students to write this way? Probably not. But I would maintain that for secondary school students in southern Africa Okara is a less harmful example of language success than many of the classic English authors whom no one living in the twentieth century should attempt to imitate anyway. Who has not seen the clumsy Victorian salutations and closing formulas appended to personal letters written by African schoolboys? I can remember one of my students in Kenya signing off with this interesting variation of colonial civil service doubletalk: "I remain, sir, your humble obedient object." Reading Okara might at least have persuaded this student that the English language is a modern, flexible instrument that can be used creatively to achieve meaningful communication. It is not a stiff, dead language clotted with ritual formulas and incomprehensible absurdities. If literature study could teach but this one lesson—that English is alive and well and living everywhere in perfect harmony with its surroundings—then it would have justified its place in the African secondary school curriculum. African literature can probably teach this lesson to Africans better than any other literature.

Cultural considerations

This brings us to the cultural argument. Here the underlying assumption is that European culture is rich while African culture is poor. The high school student who lacks exposure to Shakespeare and other English literary immortals is considered culturally deprived, mentally incomplete, badly educated, undercivilized. Even though he may live in a society totally unlike any society that ever existed anywhere in the British Isles, even though he may never again have anything to do with English culture once he finishes his schooling, it is thought he must acquire a first-hand knowledge of a few English masterpieces before he can be considered a liberally educated young man. The cultural baggage he is expected to pick up may never be of any use to him in his journey through life, but like a harlot's golden earring or a sailor's tattoo, it has come to be regarded as a necessary personal adornment without which he could not easily be identified as belonging to an *élite* group. The English classics are the foreign circumcision rites through which every African schoolboy must pass to prove his maturity.

Some educators prize the foreignness of such an educational experience. Because the books describe a different culture, they believe students will learn more from them than they would from books describing their own culture. It is rather like an ignorant nutritionist prescribing a diet of old canned foods from abroad instead of fresh local produce because he superstitiously believes all foreign foods to be more nourishing than anything that could be grown in his own back yard. He has never performed any experiments or tests to prove this; he merely assumes that the grass and vegetables are greener on the other side of the Mediterranean. He does not realize that one has to be a connoisseur with years of exotic gastronomic experience to appreciate some of the truly fine cuisine from abroad. Most African secondary school students have not developed such rarefied tastes and would prefer good, honest home cooking, which would certainly be better for them, especially in their formative years. It would be much healthier to put strange foreign dishes on the university menu rather than on every high school plate.

To overcome the prejudice Africans have been encouraged to develop against their own culture, we need to prepare a syllabus that demonstrates that Africans are not inferior to other peoples of the world, that they have customs, traditions, skills, and accomplishments of which they can be justly proud, that they need not adopt the ways of Europeans to prove themselves civilized. Indeed, they have rich civilizations of their own which have existed for a very long time and still continue to manifest great vitality. Moreover, in the past century they have become citizens of the modern world, adjusting rapidly and creatively to contacts with other peoples.

Nowhere is the creative intelligence of Africa better reflected than in African literature. The whole history of the continent can be read in the novels, plays, and poems of contemporary African writers. It is far more important that African students learn *this* history—the story of how Africa came to be what it is today, as told from an African point of view—than that they learn facts and fiction about English kings, Roman emperors, and Greek gods. Only after they have come to know themselves better by seeing accurate images in the mirror of their own literature will they be able to shed the inferiority complexes acquired from years of Western educational brain-washing. By discovering what it means to be an African in the 1970s, they will gain new self-awareness, pride, purpose, and hope for the future. Why should anyone be required to learn more about another man's culture than he knows about his own? Why should anyone be trained to believe in his own inferiority? African literature can teach Africans a true knowledge of themselves, and this is the best education any human being could possibly receive.

Political considerations
Now on to the political argument—probably the most difficult to make, given the realities of intellectual freedom in southern Africa. I do not know to what extent the censorship laws of the Republic of South Africa influence or determine the attitudes of the governments of Lesotho, Botswana, and Swaziland toward certain books and educational materials. I would assume that these governments, being independent, would be free to determine their own policies, devise their own school syllabuses, and select whatever texts seemed best suited to achieve their own educational objectives. I would assume, in other words, that books banned in South Africa would not necessarily be banned in neighboring autonomous nations and so would not automatically be excluded from consideration there as literary textbooks. This is important because some of the finest literature written by African authors, literature which would be ideal for high school classroom use, has been banned in South Africa. I am thinking of the short stories and novels of Alex La Guma; the poetry of Dennis Brutus, Arthur Nortje, and Mazisi Kunene; the autobiographical fiction of Peter Abrahams, Ezekiel Mphahlele, and Bloke Modisane—literature that speaks of South African experience in such vivid artistic terms that it sets the heart and mind afire. If we are looking for a literature that will make a difference in the lives of students in southern Africa, this is it. These works are bound to provoke an immediate aesthetic

response, for they deal honestly and effectively with things that really matter in southern Africa. They strike home because they are at home in the student's empirical universe.

Some will complain that these and similar literary works from other parts of Africa are too political, too controversial, too disagreeably propagandistic. African authors protest too much, and in so doing, drag literature down to the level of cheap polemics. The critics who make these claims (often without having read the books they condemn) tend to forget that virtually all literature protests against something, nearly every book is a piece of propaganda designed to expose some human flaw or infirmity. The only way that African literature really differs in political content from other literatures is that it happens to concern itself almost exclusively with African problems. This does not seem a valid reason for excluding it from the high school syllabus. Indeed, what could be more appropriate and educational than a book that arouses controversy about one's own way of life. The banned books question questionable social dogma and invite consideration of alternatives the authors believe would be far more humane and just. They are moral books aimed at reforming society. They make students think.

There are, of course, those who would prefer that high school students do no thinking for themselves in literature classes. These pedagogues stand behind the present system of deciphering the classics, a system of rote translation derived from educational practices of four hundred years ago when a literary education consisted of formal exercises in decoding Latin and Greek. In such a system, literature is mere language without life; the words on the page have nothing to do with the real world, which always exists somewhere outside the classroom. The student's job is simply to get right answers, not to ponder basic human questions.

Those who favor the *status quo* will naturally be the first to condemn any new approach to literature study as radical. A political approach which demands that the literature on the syllabus be relevant to the students' lives will probably be denounced with much harder words, such as "immoral,"

"objectionable," "obscene," "Communist," or "revolutionary."
I admit that the political approach I am advocating is
revolutionary, but only in the best sense of the word. I would
like to see a complete change not only in the literature syllabus
but also in the aims and methods of literature teaching at the
high school level throughout southern Africa. Introducing
teachers and students to modern African literature, particularly
modern South African literature, is one means of achieving both
ends. Using banned books which are outstanding works of
literary art is a faster means. Since such books cannot be read in
South Africa, the revolution will take somewhat longer there.
But I remain confident that with a little bit of luck and a lot of
help from the Joint Matriculation Board, the new African
literature syllabus shall overcome, even in the Republic of South
Africa.

Pedagogical considerations
The complaint that there are not enough teaching materials
available on modern African literature is nothing more than a
confession of professional incompetence. It's rather like a
dancing master asking for a pair of crutches before venturing to
learn a new step. He may be afraid of falling flat on his face but
he is not likely to gain much feeling for new movements if he
places great weight on external means of support. He must be
able to stand on his own feet or he will get nowhere himself and
will certainly be incapable of leading others in the right direction.

Actually, if he makes the smallest effort, he will find African
literature extremely easy to learn. It is not a baffling enigma
shrouded in a secret or anachronistic language. Most of it does
not require extensive interpretation. It yields itself naturally to
the African reader because it has been created by the African
writer, a cultural kinsman who shares not only a life style to some
degree analogous to the reader's but also an experience of the
English language which places similar emphasis on intelligible
communication. That is to say, because the African writer writes
in a non-African tongue, because he began writing for a

predominantly non-African audience, he has built cultural explanations into his prose so as to make his story comprehensible to the outside world. A reader does not have to be Ibo to understand Achebe, Ijaw to make sense of Okara, or Kikuyu to cope with Ngugi; these writers have already taken it upon themselves to provide whatever translations are necessary. All the reader has to do is read and react. He can throw away his cultural crutches.

For those who worry that students will continue to expect—even demand—such crutches, the challenge should be to provide them. Who is better qualified to interpret a South African literary work than a South African teacher of literature? Why should the job of discussing native-born texts be left to outsiders? I think many high school teachers in southern Africa would find it immensely fulfilling to write their own books about their own literary heritage. This would be a far more creative task than parsing the phrases of Shakespeare or supplying the footnotes to George Eliot.

And I believe students will be so enthusiastic about reading modern African literature that teaching it will be a sheer joy. There will be so much to discuss, so much that the students themselves can contribute to analysis of characters, actions, and symbols, so much that the teachers too will be excited to learn, that literature will become everyone's favorite subject. This is how literature teaching in southern Africa will be transformed from sterile exercises in classical translation to stimulating interactions with students on important issues. The literature itself will force revolutionary changes in pedagogy.

All these arguments for and against teaching African literature will remain unproven until African literary works are actually taught in the high schools of southern Africa. All we know now is that the present high school literature syllabus is unsatisfactory. This conference would not have been convened if this were not so. I believe that by modernizing and Africanizing the syllabus, we would succeed not only in improving it but also in humanizing it, making it relevant to the lives of students in southern Africa. This is a noble and worthwhile goal, for until educated men and women in this part of the world begin to learn the truth about themselves, they will forever be held in intellectual bondage by others. It is our duty as educators to teach them to listen to the sounds of a cowhide drum, the Voice of Mother Africa, so that they too may at last be free.

here English Departments Can Go

Most people are aware that English has become a world language. Indeed, this may be one of the major reasons why so many Americans do not bother to study foreign languages; they know that wherever they travel, they are likely to be able to communicate in their mother tongue. Centuries of widespread use have given English the status of an international credit card, a currency accepted almost everywhere in lieu of local mediums of exchange. Historic happenings such as the expansion of the British Empire, the emergence of the United States as a world power, the technological revolution in communications and transportation, the increase in world trade—happenings that helped to shrink the size of the globe by bringing diverse peoples into closer contact—have thus conspired to make us a nation of monoglots.

But Americans who have not traveled widely may fail to realize just how deeply the English language has sunk its roots abroad, particularly in parts of the Third World. We may be aware that Canadians, Australians, and New Zealanders grow up speaking it and that most Europeans learn it in school as a second or third language, but how many of us have observed that in nearly all the former British colonies and dependencies, English is still the language of education, government, and interstate commerce, that in places as disparate as India, Nigeria, Guyana, Sri Lanka, and Fiji it still ranks as the national language. Further, in some of these countries sizable literatures have been created by authors who have chosen to express themselves in English rather than in a native tongue. These are non-Western national literatures written in a Western international language, and they all contribute distinctive regional dimensions to a world literature written in English.

It may be difficult for Americans to conceive of a world literature written in English because the only English-language literature we tend to know anything about is the kind produced in the United Kingdom and the United States. This is what the schools and universities teach us, so this is what we accept as worthy of our attention. English departments have been exceedingly slow to recognize that England and America no longer hold a monopoly on use of the English language, that over the years substantial shares in it have been purchased by the rest of the anglophonic world.

Of course, the situation used to be even worse. Sixty years ago it was rare to find American literature being taught in American universities. English departments in those days concentrated entirely on the literature of the British Isles. However, the efforts of pioneer Americanists to win some recognition for our own literature eventually paid off; today no university English department in the United States would consider excluding American literature from its offerings.

But having won that nationalist struggle for self-recognition, can we afford to allow our English departments to continue to ignore the literatures of the rest of the English-speaking world? One might regard the fight for full recognition of such literatures as a logical extension of the American revolution in English literary studies. Having nationalized a portion of the curriculum, our objective should now be to internationalize a portion of it. Otherwise we will have won one chauvinistic battle but will have lost the wider war for expanding the horizons of university English studies. Given the fact that English is now an international literary language, why should we confine our attention to only two of the national literatures written in it? Has our half-century of farsightedness turned to myopia?

Some will answer that English literature and American literature are the most relevant ones for Americans to study, for we must understand our own heritage before we begin to investigate someone else's. This may be true if we interpret contemporary relevance in diachronic rather than synchronic terms, but if we are genuinely concerned with what is most meaningful to young Americans in the last quarter of the twentieth century, there is a lot in the traditional English syllabus that would have to be scrapped. What is the use of teaching *Sir Gawain and the Green Knight* to black teenagers when novels by Africans and West Indians that speak of the black experience elsewhere will certainly make a greater impact and lead to more significant learning? What is the point of introducing rural Texans to Chaucer, Shakespeare, Milton, or Pope when frontier sagas set in Canada, Australia, and South Africa are likely to be closer to their immediate realm of experience? Why insist that a generation brought up on soap operas and TV serials read tomes from a Great Tradition that to them seems neither great nor traditional when far more accessible popular romances from India, Nigeria, and the Philippines have the same cheap blend of sentiment, humor, and sensationalism that has always appealed to them?

If your answer to these questions is that relevance cannot be measured by proximity to the student's current interests or past experiences, then you are on my side of the argument. I agree that the familiar is not the only legitimate domain for serious study. One ought to be exposed to mind-expanding experiences as part of one's education. What better way to assure this than to immerse oneself, albeit momentarily, in another culture far removed from one's own in time, space, philosophical orientation, or material circumstances? The American student today ought to learn to be more than a patriot or cultivated Westerner; he should aim to become a citizen of the world.

If on the other hand your answer to these questions is that an understanding of our own culture ought to be the primary goal of American literary education, I shall not disagree. Only a voyeur would argue that someone else's navel is more fascinating or instructive than his own. But narcissism is not a healthy condition either. We must learn to comprehend, respect, and ultimately love our fellow man, not just our next-door neighbor or next-of-kin. If our own culture is to be given a primary place in American education, then other cultures ought to be given a secondary place rather than no place at all. Indeed, what other justification is there for studying such alien and un-American works as *The Faerie Queene, Tamburlaine, Absalom and Achitophel, Tristram Shandy,* and *Pride and Prejudice*—to name only a few revered relics from foreign graveyards that are regularly resurrected and expected to come alive in American classrooms. If we are willing to study the literature of the British Isles, we should also be willing to study the literature of other distant isles and continents, especially if that literature is presented to us in our own language.

Some will raise the objection of quality. How can we be sure that the foreign corpus is as worthy of academic embalming as our domestic corpus is assumed to be? Have any of these works attained the status of classics? How many of them have withstood the test of time? Are they really as good as, say, *Moby Dick,* Pound's *Cantos, The Great Gatsby, A Streetcar Named Desire, The Sound and the Fury, The Catcher in the Rye, Breakfast of Champions, Roots*? To answer the last question first, there are many books by foreign authors writing in English which are every bit as good and every bit as bad as the books commonly read in survey courses on contemporary American literature. Some of the better-known works from Australia, Canada, India, and South Africa, though fifty to one hundred years old, are still in print—a sure sign that they continue to interest readers. Several books written since the Second World War by West Indian and African authors already betray symptoms of literary immortality; one can say with conviction that they will endure. So one need not worry about diluting the overall strength of the syllabus by including drips from these foreign springs. If anything, the standing pool of required readings will be invigorated by their presence.

If one needs further proof, look at who is winning the literary prizes today. Writers such as V.S. Naipaul, Derek Walcott, Wilson

Harris, Doris Lessing, Nadine Gordimer, Athol Fugard, Chinua Achebe, Wole Soyinka, R.K. Narayan, Randolph Stow, Patrick White, and Margaret Laurence have all won major awards, including the Nobel Prize for Literature. Of course, one can try to belittle such recognition by pointing out that even Pearl Buck once won a Nobel Prize for Literature. But then so did Faulkner and Bellow. The Swedes aren't always wrong.

What makes our supine neglect of these internationally renowned authors so peculiar is the fact that they are already being avidly studied elsewhere in the world. University English departments in England, France, Germany, Belgium, Italy, and the Scandinavian countries regularly offer courses in "Commonwealth Literature"—another term for world literature written in English—in which works by such authors are the only books read. Similar courses are being taught in Australia, Canada, New Zealand, India, and parts of Africa, Asia, Oceania, and the Caribbean. It is strange but true that there are more students in Denmark reading these writers today than there are in all of the United States.

When are we going to catch up with the rest of the world in recognizing that English, a world language, has produced a world literature? It is time that our English departments reexamined the dimensions of the subject they profess to teach. They will discover that the field has never stopped growing and that some of its brightest flowers can now be found at the very ends of the earth.

Comparative Neglect

Comparative literature is a loose, baggy discipline with a stiff, narrow neck. International by nature, multilingual by necessity, catholic by reputation, amorphous by choice, it would seem the perfect refuge for the polyglot whose humanistic interests extend beyond the boundaries of a single culture. But when it becomes institutionalized, when degree programs are set up, when the discipline must prove its academic integrity by going through the ritual of formally disciplining its initiates, then it often loses its fabled elasticity and chokes off its own best liberal impulses. Like a dying dinosaur, it suddenly constricts, curls up into a relatively small ball, and petrifies. It is usually in this decadent phase of its development that arbitrary restrictions are placed on literary curiosity by designating certain areas of the world virtually off limits to scholarly inquiry. Students are discouraged from wandering too far away from the Eurocentric core of the curriculum. One hears echoing through the corridors the voices of graduate and undergraduate advisers raised in a dismal litany of nay-saying: "No, Mr. Smith, if you desire to do a structural comparison of Eskimo and Maori love songs, you should enroll in the Anthropology Department"; "No, Miss Jones, if you want to study Western pastoral elements in Chinese revolutionary theatre, I advise you to transfer to Oriental Languages or Theatre Arts"; "No, Mr. Wellek, if you are really intent on writing a history of African literary criticism, you had better do your degree in Linguistics or Ethnic Studies." The result is that comparative literature, ideally the most openminded discipline in any university, frequently stifles creative cross-cultural research by inhibiting the outward growth of its students. It becomes an open house with closed shutters—easy to enter, but once inside impossible to look beyond the high, claustrophobic walls. A legend over the portal reads, "Abandon scope, all ye who enter here."

I realize, of course, that not all comparative literature programs are myopically restrictive, that some even encourage students to pursue unorthodox projects well outside the mainstream of the Western tradition, but I fear that these few courageous departments tend to be the exceptions which prove the general rule—that, by and large, comparative literature studies in North American and European universities are dangerously ethnocentric, incestuously inbred, and notoriously inhospitable to scholars seriously interested in studying "exotic" non-Western literatures. I cannot prove these allegations with statistics, and I would be delighted if someone would undertake to disprove them by conducting a systematic survey of degree requirements in existing comparative literature departments in Europe, Canada, and the United States, so we could see where the truth really lies. There is much we could learn from such a survey. I would like to know, for instance, whether any real progress has been made in recent years towards liberalizing language requirements so that Arabic may be substituted for German, Tagalog for French, or Swahili for Spanish, when these or other non-European languages happen to be more relevant to a student's major research interests than any of the standard European tongues. I would also like to know if courses in non-Western literatures are required yet in any of the major comparative literature programs. For the crux of the problem, as I see it, resides in degree requirements. Whenever a department insists that all its students take certain core courses or follow roughly the same basic program of preparatory work within the department, all flexibility disappears, and the student with legitimate literary interests in what the department might regard as "fringe areas" is penalized. In my opinion the real test of any comparative literature program is its adaptability to individual needs and desires. Is the student free to do what he likes, or must the department like what he is doing? I would argue that the freer the student, the better the program.

I am not advocating the abandonment of high academic standards. The department must continue to be concerned with how well the student performs, how much he learns, and how skillfully he articulates his new knowledge. But the department—at least at the graduate level—should avoid legislating what the student must learn, and should actively encourage him to pursue his interests as far into other disciplines as he desires. In other words, an advanced comparative literature degree should be interdisciplinary, open to every kind of comparative literary investigation regardless of subject matter, intellectual orientation, or methodology, and should be specially tailored to fit the individual student's needs. There should be few, if any, required courses.

The best way to achieve this kind of latitude and flexibility, I suppose, would be to do away with comparative literature departments altogether and replace them with comparative literature committees composed of faculty from a variety of humanistic disciplines who would be willing to supervise and direct individual graduate students interested in pursuing literary research of a comparative nature. There could be a different ad hoc committee for each student, and members of the committee could meet periodically with the student and help him plan an appropriate program of study. This would seem a much more sensible arrangement than what obtains in some departments today, where students are not permitted to deviate much from a prescribed curriculum which sometimes seems designed more for the purpose of guaranteeing employment for faculty in the department than for providing students with a sound and relevant education. It may appear naive, impractical, and perhaps a bit malicious to recommend the dismantling of departments, but I can think of no alternative more likely to ensure greater freedom of choice for students. By removing unnecessary hurdles and returning the educational decision-making process to those who are being educated, comparative literature could be made the most liberal of the liberal arts.

I am speaking, I admit, from the perspective of an outcast, one whose primary scholarly preoccupations lie outside the mainstream of Western literature and therefore do not coincide with the traditional concerns of comparative literature departments. Mine may be a jaundiced view, but I see no way that my students could be properly accommodated in any but the most pliable of comparative literature programs. This I regard as a great pity, for African literatures are almost custom-made for comparative study, and it would be a great advantage for anyone working in them to have some training as a comparativist. Yet I would be most reluctant to advise someone thinking of specializing in African literatures to do his degree in comparative literature, for I suspect he would be forced to spend far too much of his time in orthodox Western literary studies and thus would not be able to develop his competence in other equally important fields such as folklore, anthropology, and African history. This is why I favor an open-ended curriculum and a degree program almost devoid of specific requirements. Comparative literature, until it evolves a structure flexible enough to serve the specialized needs of all sorts of oddballs, will remain a relatively parochial discipline.

The Teaching of African Literature in Comparative Literature Programs in the United States

Comparative literature would seem to be the ideal discipline for African literary studies. Contrastive by nature, multilingual by necessity, cross-cultural by deliberate choice, comparative literature would appear to afford the teacher and researcher lab-perfect opportunities for exploring dimensions of African literary creativity that have produced, almost simultaneously in the past half-century, a number of unique traditions of heightened verbal expression. Such intriguing phenomena as the impact of oral art on written forms, the translation of indigenous concepts into foreign tongues, the influence of Western culture on African modes of self-expression (or vice-versa), the syncretic permutation of genres, the emergence of new national literatures, and the testing of developed literary theories on rapidly developing African literary movements would offer exciting challenges to the trained comparativist as well as the comparativist-in-training. Certainly there would be no shortage of interesting topics to investigate in such a rich and variegated field. Indeed, there would be a greater likelihood of making significant discoveries on this new frontier than there would be in replowing well-mapped terrain. Comparative literature would by its very essence force fresh perspectives on data hitherto imperfectly apprehended. It would help to define the contours of the interpretive landscape, thereby generating wholly original knowledge. What more could one ask of an intellectual discipline?

Yet, unfortunately, African literature is rarely taught or studied in a comparative framework, and few of the trails that comparativists are best qualified to blaze are being satisfactorily opened up today. Part of the problem—at least in the United States, but possibly elsewhere as well—is that not many scholars are formally trained in comparative literature, and those who are tend to be very heavily committed to European literary studies. This is understandable because comparative literature, as known and practiced in the West, has been concerned almost exclusively with Western literatures, especially those located in or around Western Europe. Since comparative literature departments in American universities tend to be rather small and to be staffed with specialists borrowed from a variety of orthodox language disciplines—English, German, French, Spanish, Italian, Latin, Greek, etc.—there has been a propensity to concentrate the focus of the program on those literatures known to the faculty who volunteer or are recruited to teach comparative literature courses. Since the majority of these scholars teach European literatures, this is what the majority of the students learn. I doubt that there exists anywhere in the United States a comparative literature department in which a student could concentrate exclusively on non-Western literatures. The stranglehold of Europe on such departments is much too strong to permit this kind of wholehearted commitment to what some comparativists might regard as deviant intellectual activity. Despite the elasticity that has to be built into any comparative literature program worth its salt, there are limits to which even the most pliable program can be stretched. And those limits are set by the mental horizons of the faculty, which seldom extend much beyond Western Europe.

There are exceptions, of course. African literature has earned a place in the comparative literature curricula at Indiana University, the University of Wisconsin, the University of Southern California, the University of Washington, the University of Texas at Dallas, the University of Texas at Austin, Pennsylvania State University, and possibly a few other enlightened institutions, but this has been due almost entirely to the energetic lobbying of individuals interested in teaching African literature courses. The comparative literature departments at these universities did not actively solicit such courses because they felt their program to be deficient without them; rather, they had these courses thrust upon them by enthusiasts, some of whom may have found no other department on campus in which they could teach an "exotic" literature.

This means that a number—perhaps the majority—of scholars who teach African literature in comparative literature departments in American universities have themselves had no formal training in comparative literature per se. They are amateur comparativists sustained mainly by their wide-ranging literary interests, some of which happen to be African. Several of them have lived and taught in Africa, and a handful have done doctoral dissertations on African literature. One or two may have been dragged reluctantly into the African field during the Black Power days of the 1960s and then stayed on because they found it more exhilarating than what they had been teaching previously. But incredibly few are bona-fide comparativists.

Consequently, one is tempted to conclude that the students they teach are not receiving the best of training, but this may prove to be an erroneous assumption. A good student need not be hamstrung by the limitations of his teacher. Also, as mentioned earlier, he will not be able to devote all his time to his specialty, so he is likely to gain something useful from courses that have nothing at all to do with African literature. If he can apply this knowledge, particularly the new theoretical and methodological principles he learns, to African subject matter, he may be able to make a solid contribution to his chosen field. In other words, the second generation of African literature specialists involved in comparative literature study may turn out to be a much sturdier lot than the first. At least one can expect them to emerge from their studies with a sounder grasp of what the discipline of comparative literature is all about. The writing of a doctoral dissertation will itself ensure that the student makes use of some kind of legitimate comparative approach to the literature he has elected to examine.

The third generation of Africanist comparativists—i.e., those who will be trained by those now being trained—is likely to prove even stronger, provided their predecessors survive the rigors of contemporary academic life in the United States. One consequence of the overproduction of Ph.D.s in the 1960s and 1970s has been that it is now becoming exceedingly difficult for newly-minted Doctors in humanistic fields to find suitable jobs in American colleges and universities and even more difficult for them to keep such jobs beyond the statutory minimum number of years (usually five or six) after which they have to be moved either "up or out." Since the academic labor market in the United States is now a buyer's market, institutions have tightened up their requirements for promotion to tenure so that only those who have quite clearly proven their competence are retained. Such proof ordinarily is demanded in the form of scholarly publication, though most institutions will also consider factors such as teaching and other forms of service to the university when deciding whether to continue or terminate an appointment. Nevertheless, the old adage, "publish or perish," still holds true in American academia, and some younger scholars who have published quite a number of papers and still found themselves pushed out instead of up have complained that publication alone is no longer a guarantee of future employment, that it is now possible to publish *and* perish in many American universities, especially if one publishes in areas or journals unknown to one's colleagues. Africanists might be particularly vulnerable on this score. Unlike the situation in British or African universities, where a junior appointment can become a kind of sinecure, with promotion virtually automatic after a certain number of years regardless of scholarly performance, the American tenure system today is very much a cut-throat business with ritual executions of junior staff taking place every year, usually just before Christmas.

The system, of course, has its advantages as well as disadvantages. Only the fittest are likely to survive, and "deadwood" has little chance of perpetuating itself indefinitely in so hazardous a jungle. But on the other hand, the system tends to reward those who are able to produce fast in fields in which much work has already been done; those who labor at more basic tasks such as defining and developing a totally new field—tasks, in other words, which may require a much heavier investment of time and intellectual energy without necessarily resulting in a plethora of publications in established journals—run the risk of digging themselves an early grave in the profession. So the young comparativist committed to non-Western literature of one sort or another is an endangered species in the American academic world today; but those who survive in so cruel a system are sure to be top-notch, and they will be the teachers of tomorrow. This is why I am hopeful about the prospects for the future. While narrow may be the gate and few the number who will be admitted to the kingdom of tenured existence in American academia, the quality of such saints will be remarkably high, and the calibre of some of their acolytes possibly even higher. By the year 2000 we ought to be seeing some first-rate comparative work in African literatures coming out of American universities.

Another hopeful sign is the gradual drift towards interdisciplinary research that has become discernible in African studies circles in the United States, for this may work to the advantage of comparativists. The African Studies Association has done much to encourage this trend, first by transforming their journal, *The African Studies Review*, into a vehicle for interdisciplinary inquiry, and then by planning their 1977 annual conference as a joint meeting with the Latin American Studies Association. Comparative approaches to African literature were invited both by the editors of the ASA journal and by the conveners of the ASA/LASA conference. The 1978 ASA convention had "Traditional Medicine, Healing, and Religion" as its theme, and again literature scholars were encouraged to make their contributions by crossing disciplinary lines. The African Literature Association, at its annual meetings, has also been very hospitable to comparative and interdisciplinary perspectives, sometimes organizing panels to probe such topics as African and African-American literary relations, the interface between oral and written literatures, and anglophone, francophone, and lusophone manifestations of the same belletristic phenomenon (e.g., political protest writing, censorship, the emergence of popular literature, etc.).

But it is not only the African studies organizations that have been providing these opportunities for comparativists. The Joint Committee of the American Council of Learned Societies and the Social Science Research Council recently sponsored an interdisciplinary conference on "Cultural Transformations in Africa," to which a number of literature scholars were invited. The International Comparative Literature Association, at its triannual congresses in Bordeaux, Montreal and Innsbruck, devoted a portion of its program to consideration of Third World literatures. So did the International Federation of Modern Languages and Literatures (FILLM) at recent congresses in Sydney and Aix-en-Provence. National associations of comparative and modern literature have followed the same trend. Even the Modern Language Association, when it underwent reorganization several years ago, elevated African Literatures to the status of an independent "Section" within the Association, a status that put it on a par with other Sections such as Medieval Literature, Shakespeare, Romanticism, Twentieth-Century American Literature, etc. With all these structural changes taking place in the meeting patterns of established academic organizations, the comparativist with African literary interests certainly does not lack a forum for expressing his ideas. Indeed, he has many more opportunities for meeting with colleagues and discussing his research than he has ever had before.

These outlets are important because most American scholars working in African literatures do not find many people on their own campus with whom they can exchange ideas about subjects in which they have developed a professional interest. They tend to be loners working in a kind of intellectual isolation because their department is not likely to hire a second person to teach in the same "low-priority" area. Unless they happen to be situated at a university that has an African Studies program, they may even lack colleagues in other departments whose research or teaching activities would define them as Africanists. Forced to live in unwanted ivory-tower seclusion most of the year, such scholars need to get to conferences from time to time, if only to socialize with other hermits of the same faith.

There are certain organizations in the United States that are doing much to facilitate this kind of communication by attempting to promote an awareness of non-Western literatures among professional comparativists. One of the most effective is the Council on National Literatures led by the indefatigable Prof. Anne Paolucci of St. John's University. In 1969 she founded a biannual journal called the *Review of National Literatures* which has put out a number of special issues on "emerging and neglected" literatures of the world; a very useful African number, guest-edited by Prof. Albert Gérard of the University of Liège, appeared in 1971. She has also edited a regular newsletter, the *Council on National Literatures Report*, which has kept the scholarly community informed about such literatures, urging that they be formally studied in comparative literature programs in the United States. Further, the Council on National Literatures, under her guidance, has sponsored numerous panels and symposia on the unjustly ignored literatures of the world at annual meetings of the Modern Language Association, the American Comparative Literature Association, and various regional scholarly organizations. All this activity has generated productive discussion not only of the literatures themselves but also of the problems attendant upon teaching and studying a little-known literature in an American college or university. Though not an Africanist herself, Prof. Paolucci may have done more than any other individual to win recognition and acceptance for African literature in traditional literary disciplines, particularly in comparative literature. Her initiatives have led to a questioning of the conventional boundaries of comparative literature study.

It is on this front that the American comparativist working in African literatures must fight today. One of his most arduous professional responsibilities will be to enlighten his own colleagues, making them aware of the integrity of the field he has chosen to cultivate. He must convince them that he is not wasting his time on trivial subject matter, not mindlessly jumping on the bandwagon of the latest fad in "black studies." He must win respect for African literatures by refusing to compromise the quality of the work he does both as a scholar and as a teacher. For unless he does an absolutely first-rate job, he will be unable to persuade his peers that he is devoting his life to something significant, something of value, something far more interesting and complex than merely a fashionable, second-rate literature.

So the ultimate objective of any American comparativist working in African literatures will be to further internationalize comparative literature study in the United States. In this, he may differ significantly from his African counterpart, who may be involved in a nationalist struggle to gain recognition for African literatures within Africa itself. A comparativist teaching at an African university would be justified in seeking to place African literatures at the center of the comparative literature curriculum. In America he could only hope to win a niche somewhere on the outer fringe of his department's program. But that small foothold is well worth striving for, since it will enable a number of students to broaden their humanistic perspective. And that, after all, is what every comparative literature program should aim to do.

The Teaching of African Literature at Anglophone African Universities: An Instructive Canon

During the summer and fall of 1986 I visited twenty-six university campuses in fourteen anglophone African countries. My purpose was to pursue research on African little magazines, especially those that had been created as vehicles for writers' groups or for students and faculty at institutions of higher education. But since I was touching down at so many campuses and meeting so many colleagues who were teaching in literature and drama departments at these universities, I decided to extend the scope of my inquiry to pedagogical matters as well. I was particularly eager to learn how African literature was being taught on African campuses, what position it currently occupied in the formal curriculum, and where the most profound changes in pedagogical philosophy and practice had taken place. In other words, I was curious to discover to what extent the literature syllabus at African universities had been decolonized since independence. And I wanted to know the specifics of this transformation—not just the record of major structural adjustments but also the interesting little details contained in course descriptions and reading lists. Which authors and which texts were students now required to study? Why were these particular books selected? And what could such data tell us about the process of canon formation in African literature studies today?

Not all the institutions I visited were able to supply all the documents I was seeking. Some universities were on their long vacation when I passed through; some departments had not yet duplicated the course descriptions and reading lists prepared by their faculty for the coming year; some campus bookshops or registrar's offices had no up-to-date university calendars or annuals for sale; some institutions had operated for years without printing and circulating such documents; and some departmental chairmen probably suspected me of working for the CIA or, worse yet, for a radical faction within the department intent on destabilizing and further deanglicizing the traditional English syllabus. But helpful colleagues nearly everywhere in my five-month journey supplied me with whatever documents they could lay their hands on or else sent them to me after I had returned home. I also solicited such materials from more than a dozen institutions I was not able to visit, and I have tried to fill in gaps in the documentary record by consulting catalogues from African universities received by American and British libraries. Consequently, I now have reliable data on African literature teaching at 30 of the 40 universities in anglophone Africa (including the University of Yaoundé in Cameroon, but excluding—for a variety of reasons—all the universities in the Republic of South Africa). However, since 10 of the 40 institutions approached have not yet responded to my requests for information, and since I possess incomplete data from several of those that did respond, my survey obviously is far from complete. Nonetheless, it may be of some use to report my findings here, if only to give palpable evidence of what I am attempting to do. This may help to allay unnecessary suspicions and thereby persuade the keepers of invisible records to release their stream of data into my half-filled standing pool.

The data received may appear weighted toward West Africa, especially Nigeria, but this imbalance only reflects reality. More than sixty percent (i.e., 25 out of 40) of the universities in anglophone Africa are located in West Africa, and 68 percent of those in West Africa (17 out of 25) are in Nigeria. If anything, Nigeria, with 13 of 17 universities reporting, is slightly underrepresented in the present data pool, but the region least satisfactorily represented is East Africa, with four universities (out of 9) in Kenya, Uganda, and Sudan not yet reporting, and the University of Dar es Salaam offering descriptions of only a few of its drama and literature courses. Central and Southern Africa, on the other hand, are almost fully covered, with only the University of Malawi deficient in supplying comprehensive data.

What we have, then, is information on 194 courses taught at 30 universities in 14 African nations, a sample representing perhaps as much as 60 per cent of the total number of African literature courses taught in anglophone Africa in the mid-1980s. This averages out to more than six courses per campus, with several universities offering more than a dozen courses each and a few offering only one or two or three courses each. The sample embraces graduate as well as undergraduate curricula, courses that focus exclusively on African texts as well as those that treat African and non-African texts together, and courses that cover oral forms of literature as well as those concerned entirely with written literature. These 194 courses can be subdivided into generic and topical categories as follows:

Genres

Fiction	31
Short Story	4
Prose	2
Drama	22
Poetry	23
Combined genres (drama and poetry)	5
Children's literature	2
Oral literature	11
Criticism	6
TOTAL	106

Topics

The first conclusion that can be drawn from this mass of data is that African literature now occupies a significant place in the English program of most anglophone African universities. The majority of these universities have retained Departments of English under one nomenclature or another, but a few, notably those in Kenya, Tanzania, and Zambia, have chosen to subsume such departments under a larger rubric by renaming them Departments of Literature, thus opening the way for a major transformation of the syllabus. The University of Sokoto in Nigeria includes English studies as one branch in a Department of European Languages, and the University of Asmara does much the same, placing it in a Department of Foreign Languages. Only the University of Yaoundé in Cameroon has established a separate Department of African Literature, and at the other extreme only the University of Mauritius avoids teaching African literature altogether. The most radical reorientations of literature study have taken place at universities in Kenya and Tanzania, while the staunchest conservatism has been maintained by English Departments at the University of Ghana and the University of the Cape Coast, resulting in only minor alterations of the old colonial curriculum. Yet though wide differences may be discernible from one region to the next or even from one institution to the next, it is quite clear that African universities have not been slow to recognize that African literature merits serious study and ought to be made available to students seeking a broad liberal education. The decolonization of literature study in Africa is thus already well under way.

If we look more closely at the work required of students who take African literature courses, we observe some interesting reading patterns. In these 194 courses, works by 226 different authors were assigned, 97 of these authors being read in only one course (out of the 194), 31 in two courses, 24 in three courses, 19 in four courses, 22 in five to nine courses, and the remaining 34 in ten or more courses. The most popular assigned author was Wole Soyinka, whose works were used in 87 different courses, or around 47 percent of the total number of courses. He was followed closely by Ngugi wa Thiong'o, whose works were used in 77 different courses (about 42%), and then by Chinua Achebe, whose works featured in 57 courses (about 30%). Further back but still conspicuous by the frequency of their appearance were J.P. Clark, Ayi Kwei Armah, Okot p'Bitek, and Alex La Guma, each of whom was represented in between 29 to 36 of the courses surveyed (roughly 15 to 19 percent of the total). Thereafter the percentages dropped off rather sharply, but Ousmane Sembène, Athol Fugard, Peter Abrahams, Léopold Senghor, Christopher Okigbo, Ola Rotimi, Mongo Beti, Ama Ata Aidoo, and Dennis Brutus made quite respectable showings, and the remaining seventeen of the statistically prominent literary personalities averaged between ten and eighteen appearances (roughly 5 to 9 percent) on the 194 reading lists examined.

But there are other variables in the data base that need to be considered too. Several authors, especially the top four—namely, Soyinka, Ngugi, Achebe, and Armah—occasionally had more than one book assigned in a single course. In addition, some authors were read in more institutions than others, though not necessarily in more courses. Some were also read in more nations than others, though not necessarily in more institutions or more courses. To give these variables the statistical significance they deserve, I have devised a Better Ultimate Rating Plan that takes into account not only an author's frequency of assignment but also his geographical and institutional spread. He or she achieves a numerical score in each of four categories: number of books assigned, number of courses prescribing these books, number of institutions offering these courses, and number of nations housing institutions offering courses that prescribe these books.

The four individual sums are then dispassionately added together into one grand total for each writer and those compound sums help us to sort out the somebodies from the nobodies in African literature studies and to place each writer with more precision on a hierarchical scale of relative importance. Here is a chart summarizing the results achieved through the kind of objective quantification that the Better Ultimate Rating Plan makes possible:

	Authors	Books	Courses	Institutions	Nations	Totals
1.	Soyinka	146	87	30	14	277
2.	Ngugi	110	77	28	13	228
3.	Achebe	71	57	27	12	167
4.	Armah	47	33	21	10	111
5.	Clark	44	36	20	9	109
6.	Okot	41	31	23	12	107
7.	La Guma	35	29	18	8	90
8.	Sembène	33	26	15	10	83
9.	Fugard	24	24	20	11	79
10.	Senghor	22	21	17	9	69
11.	Beti	24	20	16	8	68
12.	Abrahams	23	21	14	9	67
13.	Brutus	25	20	15	6	66
14.	Okigbo	21	21	15	8	65
15.	Aidoo	21	20	16	7	64
16.	Rotimi	20	20	13	6	59
17.	Okara	18	18	13	8	57
18.	Awoonor	17	16	13	6	52
19.	Oyono	15	15	11	7	48
20.	Githae-Mugo*	17	17	14	7	45
21.	Laye	12	12	11	7	42
	Mphahlele	13	13	10	6	42
	Sutherland	14	14	9	5	42
24.	Mwangi	12	11	9	5	37
25.	Lessing	13	11	6	5	35
	Ngugi wa Mirii*	10	10	8	7	35
	Osofisan	14	12	8	1	35
28.	D. Diop	10	10	8	6	34
29.	Al-Hakim	11	10	8	4	33

	Amadi	10	10	9	4	33
	Bâ	10	10	9	4	33
	Peters	12	9	9	3	33
33.	Okpewho	11	10	8	5	32
34.	Head	12	8	6	5	31
35.	Nkosi	8	8	7	4	27
36.	Kunene	7	7	7	5	26
	Mtshali	7	7	7	5	26
38.	Angira	8	8	6	3	25
	Marechera	10	7	4	4	25

*Co-author with Ngugi wa Thiong'o

Before we jump to too many conclusions based on the arithmetical elegance of this Better Ultimate Rating Plan, a few natural biases in the measuring instrument need to be mentioned. First, these results are based on book lists, and when the books included on such lists are composite works (anthologies, for instance), it is impossible to determine from a citation of the title alone exactly which authors in that text are actually assigned for reading in class. Since most poetry courses in Africa tend to be taught via anthologies, one could argue that poets are thus likely to be ranked lower in the final tally than they should be. On the other hand, it could be argued with equal cogency that anthologized poets don't deserve any higher ranking merely because they happen to be among a large gang of poets read; a teacher may spend only a few minutes discussing individual poems in an anthology whereas he might take several hours to discuss a whole novel or play. Certainly Okot p'Bitek, Léopold Senghor, Dennis Brutus, and Christopher Okigbo, poets whose major works have been published in book form and therefore have been available in their entirety for more sustained scrutiny in the classroom, have not fared badly in the final tally, being ranked sixth, tenth, thirteenth, and fourteenth respectively. Other part-time poets—Soyinka, Achebe, Clark, Awoonor, and Okara, for instance—don't appear to have suffered much neglect as poets either. So it may be only the minor bards, those a teacher might be tempted to survey rather than deal with intensively, who have scored in the lower numbers on the Better Ultimate Rating Plan, and they probably deserve to be relegated to the minor leagues.

Another possible bias is one that would tend to favor the author who does not specialize in one genre but writes in several—Soyinka, for example, or Ngugi. However, it is necessary to recognize a qualitative criterion at work here too. There are some prolific authors writing in various genres whose works seldom are adopted for use in university classrooms. These energetic scribblers do not appear to have achieved any edge over others simply because they express themselves in a variety of forms. Perhaps it is only the greatest of the multi-talented authors who are being read in the greatest multitude of courses; leading artists such as Soyinka, Ngugi, Achebe and Clark may really merit close study in whatever form they write, so their final high ranking may derive as much from their overall reputation as from their versatility. One does not necessarily read a bad poet because he happens to be a good novelist.

Nonetheless, it is no doubt fair to say that all else being equal, an excellent author who has written many books is likely to end up with a higher score on the Better Ultimate Rating Plan than an excellent author who has written only one. In a university English program it is possible to make productive use of a single text only a limited number of times; one cannot assign it in every course in which it might fit. A better strategy is to select a second or third book by that same author rather than go on teaching a text the students already know. So prolific writers of quality works may have an advantage over their less productive peers. Indeed, Okigbo is the only author in our survey to have made it into the top twenty on the strength of a single extant text.

There may also be a minor bias in our rating scheme resulting from the nationality or even the ethnicity of an author. Most African university English departments display an understandable preference for teaching local literature (i.e., literature produced by native sons and daughters), and sometimes there are special courses set up to survey the national or regional literary output—"Zimbabwean Literature" at the University of Zimbabwe, "Nigerian Literature" at various Nigerian campuses, "Southern African Literature" at the University of Lesotho, for instance. In fact, more than half of the authors read in only one or two courses out of the total corpus of 194 are local or regional products, authors specially selected to appeal to indigenous interests. The same bias may occur in other courses that do not have an explicit geographical focus. At the University of Calabar, for instance, nine of twelve authors included in a second-year survey of African prose (ELS 2011) are Nigerian, and three of these happen to teach at the University of Calabar! Such nationalism (some might prefer to brand it parochialism or curricular nepotism) could lead to bigger scores for native sons and daughters who hail from nations having a lot of universities—Nigeria, for instance.

But an author would need a truly international reputation to achieve a top score in the Better Ultimate Rating Plan. A relatively new writer such as Femi Osofisan, for example, makes quite a respectable showing in Nigeria, where his works are taught in twelve courses at eight different universities (out of the thirteen Nigerian institutions surveyed to date), but since they are taught nowhere else in anglophone Africa, his total score comes to only 35, which places him in a three-way tie for the twenty-fifth spot among the front-runners.

Osofisan may have deliberately opted for national rather than international fame by publishing most of his books with local Nigerian firms, and there may be other authors equally talented who do not show up at all among the highest-scoring three dozen in the Better Ultimate Rating Plan's sweepstakes for much the same reason: their books are not widely available throughout Africa. Indeed, it is instructive to note how many of the top scorers are published exclusively or largely by Heinemann Educational Books in the famous African Writers Series or by other firms with good pan-African or regional distribution (e.g., Oxford University Press for much of Soyinka, Clark, Fugard, and

Senghor; East African Publishing House and Heinemann East African for some of Ngugi, Okot, and Armah). In fact, quite a few of the 194 course reading lists examined in this survey might change considerably in the future if a greater variety of literary texts were available for adoption as set books. Many teachers told me that when they plan a course, they have an ideal syllabus in mind but they are forced to modify it because a number of the texts they would like to use simply cannot be obtained or else are too costly for students to purchase; in these circumstances some have resorted to teaching books acquired in multiple copies years ago by their university library. The ideal syllabus thus gives way to a practical syllabus, one that relies on older texts mixed with inexpensive books published locally. The classroom becomes not a marketplace of the best ideas but a marketplace of whatever ideas are within arm's reach. So another bias in the data base derives from the very nature of the data collected: the Better Ultimate Rating Plan measures only the real, not the ideal.

When we analyze the data by text rather than by author, some interesting patterns emerge. We find that of the 452 different texts used in the 194 courses surveyed, 208 were assigned in only one course, 99 in two, 41 in three, 52 in four to six, and the remaining 52 in seven or more. Relying on the same method of adding together the number of courses, institutions, and nations in which a text is used, here is a ranked list of books that teachers of African literature at African universities evidently regard as worthiest of their students' attention:

BETTER ULTIMATE RATING PLAN (TEXTS)

Books by Author & Title	Courses	Institutions	Nations	Totals
1. Achebe, *Arrow of God*	23	16	7	46
2. Ngugi, *A Grain of Wheat*	22	15	7	44
3. Ngugi, *Petals of Blood*	19	15	7	44
4. Achebe, *A Man of the People*	19	14	8	41
5. Okot, *Song of Lawino*	19	14	7	40
6. Nugui/Githae-Mugo, *Trial of Dedan Kimathi*	18	14	7	39
7. Armah, *Beautyful Ones...*	17	12	7	36

Soyinka, *The Interpreters*	16	13	7	36
9. Soyinka, *Kongi's Harvest*	13	12	8	33
10. Okigbo, *Labyrinths*	15	11	6	32
11. Sembène, *God's Bits of Wood*	13	10	8	31
12. Achebe, *Things Fall Apart*	13	10	7	30
13. Soyinka, *Idanre*	14	10	5	29
14. Ngugi/Ngugi, *I Will Marry...*	10	9	7	25
La Guma, *Walk in the Night*	11	10	4	25
Fugard, *Statements*	9	9	7	25
17. Sutherland, *Marriage of Anansewa*	11	8	5	24
18. Bâ, *So Long a Letter*	10	9	4	23
Beti, *Poor Christ of Bomba*	9	8	6	23
20. Armah, *Fragments*	10	8	4	22
21. Sembène, *Xala*	9	7	5	21
Armah, *2000 Seasons*	10	7	4	21
La Guma, *In the Fog...*	10	7	4	21
24. Ngugi, *Devil on the Cross*	9	7	4	20
Okara, *Fisherman's Invocation*	8	8	4	20
Brutus, *Letters to Martha*	9	8	3	20
Oyono, *Old Man and the Medal*	8	7	5	20
28. Beti, *Mission to Kala*	8	7	4	19
Ngugi, *The River Between*	8	8	3	19
Soyinka, *Lion and the Jewel*	7	6	6	19
Oyono, *Houseboy*	7	7	5	19
32. Rotimi, *Gods Are Not to Blame*	8	6	4	18
Achebe, *Morning Yet...*	7	6	5	18
Brutus, *A Simple Lust*	8	7	3	18
Clark, *Song of a Goat*	7	7	4	18
36. Soyinka, *Shuttle in the Crypt*	8	7	2	17
La Guma, *Time of the Butcherbird*	6	6	5	17
Soyinka, *Collected Plays*	6	6	5	17
Okara, *The Voice*	7	5	5	17
Soyinka, *Madmen and Specialists*	8	7	2	17
Aidoo, *Anowa*	7	7	3	17

Cumulatively, Ngugi now occupies the highest position, with three books in the top ten. Achebe and Soyinka come next with two each, followed by Okot, Armah, and Okigbo, in that order. Soyinka doesn't put in an appearance until *The Interpreters* ties for seventh and *Kongi's Harvest* takes the ninth spot, but this may not reflect the true position of his best dramatic work, for his *Collected Plays* turns up later on the list in a tie for thirty-sixth, and had the individual plays in those two volumes been identified by title, some of them no doubt would have stood higher in the final numerical ranking. But it is probably fair to conclude from the evidence now before us that while there appears to be widespread agreement about which are the most important works produced by Ngugi, Achebe, Okot, Armah, Okigbo, and Sembène, no such unanimity exists as far as Soyinka's output is concerned. The other great writers are identified with one or two masterpieces, but there is some confusion about what Soyinka's major contributions to African literature have been. He has no fewer than seven titles among the top three dozen, four of them dramatic pieces, yet his highest ranking work is a novel and his third highest is a collection of poems. From this evidence we may be forced to conclude that while there is a clear consensus among African university teachers that Soyinka is Africa's most significant writer, there is still disagreement about which text or texts may be regarded as his most significant writings. He may be a master craftsman with no single universally accepted masterpiece to his name. Or another way of putting it would be to say that while he is a jack of all genres, he is a king or ace of none.

A few years ago I introduced another mathematical model for measuring the reputation of African authors—something I called the Famous Authors' Reputation Text. This was basically a citation index which recorded the frequency with which anglophone African authors were discussed in books and articles on African literature. My underlying assumption was that authors discussed frequently by literary critics were held in higher esteem than those seldom discussed. The Famous Authors' Reputation Test thus attempted a quantitative solution to a qualitative riddle, arriving at scores that could be compared to other scores on a calibrated scale ranging from highest literary worth to total worthlessness. How do the results from the Famous Authors' Reputation Test stack up against those from the Better Ultimate Rating Plan? Are there writers who score higher with the critics than they do with the teachers, or vice versa? Where do the largest discrepancies lie? I am appending one last chart documenting the relative standing of the major writers in each list and then, again through simple arithmetic, combining their standings in both lists to produce a final cumulation that reveals who are the top twenty-one writers in anglophone Africa today, at least according to teachers at African universities and literary critics worldwide. Since francophone, Arabic, and white African writers were not included in the Famous Authors' Reputation Test, I have omitted them from this version of the Better Ultimate Rating Plan to iron out a conspicuous new wrinkle in the data base and to ensure greater uniformity in the final results. However, I have been unable to delete the non-African critical input from the Famous Authors' Reputation Test, so the two data bases are not perfectly symmetrical racially. Nor are they symmetrical temporally, since the Famous Authors' Reputation Test is a diachronic measure covering literary criticism written over a fifty-one year span (1936-1986) and the Better Ultimate Rating Plan is a synchronic measure covering teaching practices in the mid-1980s only. Yet as crude measuring instruments, these two imperfect tools—used either individually or together—may still serve us well enough for large-scale calibrational and comparative purposes. We may not be able to make fine discriminations with them, but we should be able to discern dominant patterns and arrive at fairly accurate gross distinctions. Until someone devises a more sophisticated gauge using basically the same kinds of empirical data, this may be the closest we can ever come to determining the true canon of African literature today.

FAMOUS AUTHORS' REPUTATION TEST	BETTER ULTIMATE RATING PLAN	COMBINED RANKINGS
1. Soyinka 2961	1. Soyinka 277	1. Soyinka 2
2. Achebe 2463	2. Ngugi 228	2. Achebe 5
3. Ngugi 1657	3. Achebe 167	Ngugi 5
4. Armah 643	4. Armah 111	4. Armah 8
5. Clark 608	5. Clark.................... 109	5. Clark............ 10
6. Tutuola 590	6. Okot 107	6. Okot.............. 15
7. Ekwensi 528	7. La Guma 90	7. Okigbo 18
8. Okigbo 463	8. Abrahams 67	8. Abrahams 19
9. Okot 453	9. Brutus 66	9. Brutus 21
10. Mphahlele .. 428	10. Okigbo 65	La Guma 21
11. Abrahams... 419	11. Aidoo 64	11. Okara 26
12. Brutus 396	12. Rotimi 59	Mphahlele.... 26
13. Okara 357	13. Okara 57	13. Awoonor 29
14. La Guma 355	14. Awoonor 52	Rotimi 29
15. Awoonor 345	15. Githae-Mugo* 45	15. Aidoo 30
16. Head 295	16. Mphahlele 42	16. Tutuola 36
17. Rotimi 266	Sutherland........... 42	17. Ekwensi 40
18. Emecheta 234	18. Mwangi 37	Head 40
19. Aidoo 229	19. Ngugi wa Mirii* . 35	19. Amadi 41
20. Amadi 181	Osofisan 35	20. Osofisan 45
21. Aluko 174	21. Amadi 33	21. Emecheta 49
22. Liyong 171	Peters 33	22. Sutherland ...50
23. Farah 156	23. Okpewho 32	23. Peters............ 51
24. Nwapa 151	24. Head.................... 31	24. Mwangi........ 54
25. Equiano 147	25. Nkosi.................... 27	25. Mtshali 57
26. Osofisan 138	26. Mtshali 26	26. Nkosi 62
27. Omotoso 133	Kunene................. 26	
28. Plaatje 127	28. Angira 25	
29. Ogot 126	Marechera............. 25	
30. Peters 125	30. Tutuola 23	
31. Mtshali........ 121	31. Serumaga............. 21	
32. Nzekwu 113	Emecheta 21	
33. Munonye 106	33. Ntiru..................... 17	
34. Mazrui 105	Ekwensi 17	
Sutherland . 105		
36. Mwangi 104		
37. Nkosi 101	*Co-author with Ngugi wa Thiong'o	

What now appears quite obvious is that teachers have a far greater interest in La Guma, Aidoo, Rotimi, Sutherland, and Mwangi than critics do, while critics tend to be much more fascinated with Tutuola, Ekwensi, Mphahlele, Head, Aluko, and Liyong than teachers are. Okot, Abrahams, and Brutus are also great favorites with teachers and are only slightly less admired by critics, while Soyinka, Achebe, Ngugi, Clark, Okigbo, Okara, and Amadi seem to be about equally popular with both sets of interpreters. In some respects the rankings in the Famous Authors' Reputation Test and the Better Ultimate Rating Plan do not differ a great deal, and in the final analysis more or less the same names rise to the top in small elite groups in both measures. Soyinka, Achebe and Ngugi remain the presiding triumvirate, supported by a strong second five consisting of Armah, Clark, Okot, Okigbo, and Abrahams. Next come seven middle men and women (Brutus, La Guma, Okara, Mphahlele, Awoonor, Rotimi, Aidoo), then four penultimates (Tutuola, Ekwensi, Head, Amadi), and finally seven laggards (Osofisan, Emecheta, Sutherland, Peters, Mwangi, Mtshali, Nkosi) who are low enough on the combined list to be challenged by upwardly mobile newcomers and downwardly mobile old has-beens.

The canon, in other words, is still in a state of creative gestation; hardly anything about it is permanently fixed and immutable. Only the top three names on the final list appear to be in an unassailable position, and after them only the next five seem relatively secure in their standing for the foreseeable future. The rest may be merely canon-fodder—here today, gone tomorrow, and ignored twenty or two hundred and twenty years hence by literary critics and teachers alike. Such is the toll exacted by time, which allows only the sturdiest monuments to survive. Africa, a young literary culture, may not yet have yielded up her most durable treasures to posterity. The best may be those classics yet to come.

Big Shots and Little Shots of the Canon

Since 1985 I have been filling some of my free hours with arithmetical games aimed at establishing reliable statistical methods for ranking anglophone African authors in a hierarchical scale that reveals their standing, past and present, in the eyes of the public and in relation to their peers. One could say that I have been playing with numbers in order to address seriously those questions of taste and discrimination on which everyone has warm opinions but no one has cold, hard facts. To put it another way, I have been employing simple mathematics in an effort to discover scientifically and without trace of subjective bias, the configuration of the anglophone African literary canon, today and yesterday, with all its pillars, monuments, pedestals, niches, notches, and small holes in the wall neatly arranged in their proper places and faithfully recorded in the order of their importance. Please note that I have said I have been trying to *discover* the canon, not to invent it or to construct it. And I assure you that there is no way I can skew it so that my own favorite authors stand higher on the sliding scale than they should. Pure, unvarnished numerical data make it impossible for me or anyone else to tamper with the evidence and produce compromised results. These statistics cannot lie, for they repose on a bedrock of sheer calculation, made with precision on the finest Japanese pocket calculators, and set down with Olympian disinterest in an atmosphere of utmost tranquillity, not unlike the ambiance in that chamber of heaven where God sits, dispassionately paring his (or her) fingernails.

How does this numbers game work? Let me explain it succinctly, with the aid of a few charts. My first measuring instrument, called the Famous Authors' Reputation Test (Lindfors 1990), consisted of nothing more than a simple citation index that recorded the frequency with which an author and his (or her) works were discussed in detail in print by literary scholars and critics. Points were awarded not only for frequency of citation but also for relative size of citation, with every author receiving three points for each book or article devoted exclusively to him or her, and one point for every cross-reference—that is, for every appearance of significant length (i.e., a page or more of critical commentary) in a book or article devoted to two or more writers. A mere mention in a quick survey of a large group of writers counted for nothing at all. A writer had to be discussed in roughly 300 to 500 words or more to earn one point, but the most he or she could garner from a single critical source, even if it was a doctoral dissertation of a thousand pages explicating the nuances in one line of haiku verse, was three points. In other words, frequency of substantive citation counted for more than the longwindedness of a sole, fanatical admirer. And to score big, one had to win points across the board, not just routine encomiums from friends in one's own literary coterie. The Famous Authors' Reputation Test measured fame as well as reputation.

The sources from which statistical data were gleaned in my quest for meaningful numbers were the three successive bibliographies I compiled and published under the title *Black African Literature in English* (hereafter cited as BALE). The first volume, covering the years 1936-76, contained 3305 entries; the second, covering five additional years (1977-81), contained 2831 entries; and the third, another five-year supplement extending coverage from 1982 through 1986, contained 5689 entries. So the total body of data came to 11,825 entries representing 51 years of critical commentary on anglophone African literature. This was not a small or selective data base. On the contrary, it was meant to be as comprehensive as possible.

TABLE ONE

Authors	BALE I (1936-76)				BALE II (1977-81)				BALE III (1982-86)				GRAND TOTALS			
	E	CR	RT	WT	E	CR	RT	WT	E	CR	RT	WT	E	CR	RT	WT
Abrahams	40	69	109	189	21	29	50	92	31	45	76	138	92	143	235	419
Achebe	185	309	494	864	190	151	341	721	216	230	446	878	591	690	1281	2463
Armah	25	77	102	152	27	68	95	149	80	102	182	342	132	247	379	643
Awoonor	16	64	80	112	21	31	52	94	28	55	83	139	65	150	215	345
Brutus	26	35	61	113	16	25	41	73	52	54	106	210	94	114	208	396
Clark	30	154	184	244	17	52	69	103	49	114	163	261	96	320	416	608
Ekwensi	36	116	152	224	23	40	63	109	42	69	111	195	101	225	326	528
La Guma	14	49	63	91	12	30	42	66	50	48	98	198	76	127	203	355
Mphahlele	26	73	99	151	22	48	70	114	34	61	95	163	82	182	264	428
Ngugi	43	98	141	227	129	108	237	495	242	209	451	935	414	415	829	1657
Okara	16	111	127	159	7	43	50	64	21	71	92	134	44	225	269	357
Okigbo	39	91	130	208	16	41	57	89	39	49	88	166	94	181	275	463
Okot	30	42	72	132	20	45	65	105	55	51	106	216	105	138	243	453
Soyinka	175	280	455	805	144	168	312	600	418	312	730	1566	737	760	1497	2971
Tutuola	55	123	178	288	28	47	75	131	42	45	87	171	125	215	340	590

E=Entry
CR=Cross-reference
RT=Raw total
WT=Weighted total

The rows of numbers on the accompanying tables should now begin to make some sense. If, for example, we look at the first set of columns under BALE I in Table One, we see that between 1936 and 1976 there were 40 books and articles (in column E for entry) devoted exclusively to Peter Abrahams as well as 69 additional sources in which he was discussed at significant length (in column CR for cross-reference). If we add these two figures together, we get a raw total (RT) of 109, but if we add weight to the discrete entries by multiplying them by a factor of three, we get a weighted total (WT) of 189, which may be a truer index of his standing than if we were to make no distinction between entries and cross-references. To put the matter in the form of arithmetical equations, we could state that E + CR = RT and that 3E + CR = WT. If we do the same for the supplementary volumes, BALE II and BALE III, and then add up the results, we arrive at the grand totals in the fourth set of columns on the right, totals which show us where Abrahams's numbers stood after slightly more than half a century of academic critical activity.

TABLE TWO

BALE I

	E		CR		RT (E+CR)		WT (3E+CR)	
1.	Achebe	185	Achebe	309	Achebe	494	Achebe	864
2.	Soyinka	175	Soyinka	280	Soyinka	455	Soyinka	805
3.	Tutuola	55	Clark	154	Clark	184	Tutuola	288
4.	Ngugi	43	Tutuola	123	Tutuola	178	Clark	244
5.	Abrahams	40	Ekwensi	116	Ekwensi	152	Ngugi	227
6.	Okigbo	39	Okara	111	Ngugi	141	Ekwensi	224
7.	Ekwensi	36	Ngugi	98	Okigbo	130	Okigbo	208
8.	Clark }	30	Okigbo	91	Okara	127	Abrahams	189
	Okot							
9.			Armah	77	Abrahams	109	Okara	159
10.	Brutus }	26	Mphahlele	73	Armah	102	Armah	152
	Mphahlele							
11.			Abrahams	69	Mphahlele	99	Mphahlele	151
12.	Armah	25	Nzekwu*	65	Awoonor	80	Okot	132
13.	Awoonor }	16	Awoonor	64	Okot	72	Brutus	113
	Okara							
14.			Aluko*	50	Nzekwu*	69	Awoonor	112
15.	Liyong*	15	La Guma	49	La Guma	63	La Guma	91

BALE II

	E		CR		RT (E+CR)		WT (3E+CR)	
1.	Achebe	190	Soyinka	168	Achebe	341	Achebe	721
2.	Soyinka	144	Achebe	151	Soyinka	312	Soyinka	600
3.	Ngugi	129	Ngugi	108	Ngugi	237	Ngugi	495
4.	Tutuola	28	Armah	68	Armah	95	Armah	149
5.	Armah	27	Clark	52	Tutuola	75	Tutuola	131
6.	Ekwensi	23	Mphahlele	48	Mphahlele	70	Mphahlele	114
7.	Mphahlele	22	Tutuola	47	Clark	69	Ekwensi	109
8.	Abrahams } Awoonor	21	Okot	45	Okot	65	Okot	105
9.			Okara	43	Ekwensi	63	Clark	103
10.	Okot	20	Okigbo	41	Okigbo	57	Awoonor	94
11.	Head[*]	18	Ekwensi	40	Awoonor	52	Abrahams	92
12.	Clark Emecheta[*] Plaatje[*]	17	Awoonor	31	Abrahams } Okara	50	Okigbo	89
13.			La Guma	30			Brutus	73
14.			Abrahams	29	La Guma	42	La Guma	66
15.	Brutus } Okigbo	16	Aidoo[*]	26	Brutus	41	Head[*]	65

BALE III

	E		CR		RT (E+CR)		WT (3E+CR)	
1.	Soyinka	418	Soyinka	312	Soyinka	730	Soyinka	1566
2.	Ngugi	242	Achebe	230	Ngugi	451	Ngugi	935
3.	Achebe	216	Ngugi	209	Achebe	446	Achebe	878
4.	Armah	80	Clark	114	Armah	182	Armah	342
5.	Head*	58	Armah	102	Clark	163	Clark	261
6.	Okot	55	Okara	71	Ekwensi	111	Head* } Okot	216
7.	Brutus	52	Ekwensi	69	Rotimi*	108		
8.	La Guma	50	Rotimi*	65	Brutus } Okot	106	Brutus	210
9.	Clark	49	Mphahlele	61			La Guma	198
10.	Rotimi*	43	Awoonor	55	Head*	100	Ekwensi	195
11.	Ekwensi } Tutuola	42	Brutus	54	La Guma	98	Rotimi*	194
12.			Okot	51	Mphahlele	95	Tutuola	171
13.	Emecheta*	41	Okigbo	49	Okara	92	Emecheta*	170
14.	Okigbo	39	La Guma	48	Emecheta* } Okigbo	88	Okigbo	166
15.	Mphahlele	34	Aidoo } Emecheta*	47			Mphahlele	163

GRAND TOTALS

	E		CR		RT (E+CR)		WT (3E+CR)	
1.	Soyinka	737	Soyinka	760	Soyinka	1497	Soyinka	2961
2.	Achebe	591	Achebe	690	Achebe	1281	Achebe	2463
3.	Ngugi	414	Ngugi	415	Ngugi	829	Ngugi	1657
4.	Armah	132	Clark	320	Clark	416	Armah	643
5.	Tutuola	125	Armah	247	Armah	379	Clark	608
6.	Okot	105	Ekwensi } Okara	225	Tutuola	340	Tutuola	590
7.	Ekwensi	101			Ekwensi	326	Ekwensi	528
8.	Clark	96	Tutuola	215	Okigbo	275	Okigbo	463
9.	Brutus } Okigbo	94	Mphahlele	182	Okara	269	Okot	453
10.			Okigbo	181	Mphahlele	264	Mphahlele	428
11.	Abrahams	92	Awoonor	150	Okot	243	Abrahams	419
12.	Mphahlele	82	Abrahams	143	Abrahams	235	Brutus	396
13.	Head*	79	Okot	138	Awoonor	215	Okara	357
14.	La Guma	76	La Guma	127	Brutus	208	La Guma	355
15.	Awoonor	65	Brutus	114	La Guma	203	Awoonor	345

E=Entry
CR=Cross-reference
RT=Raw total
WT=Weighted total
GWT=Grand weighted total

Table Two performs basically the same function as Table One, but the columns have been arranged in numerical rather than alphabetical order so that one can see more easily who stood where in each category in each volume. The WT column in the grand totals (the last column on the right in the final cumulation) is the important one, giving the relative positions of the fifteen most frequently studied anglophone African authors. As far as scholars and critics are concerned, this is the canon, or at least this is the very top of the canon. Respectable scores ranging from 300 to 100 points in the grand weighted total (GWT) have been earned by 21 additional authors who collectively could perhaps be designated as major minor writers.

TABLE THREE

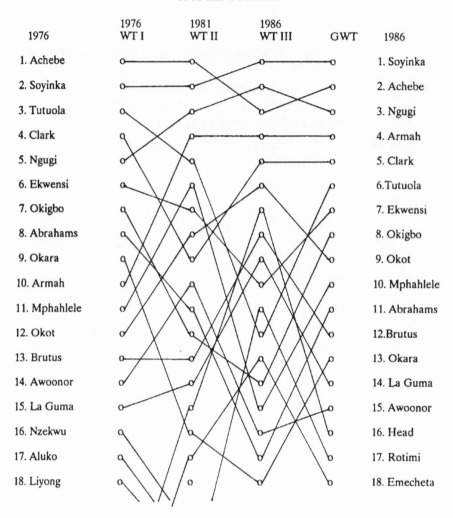

1976	1976 WT I	1981 WT II	1986 WT III	GWT	1986
1. Achebe					1. Soyinka
2. Soyinka					2. Achebe
3. Tutuola					3. Ngugi
4. Clark					4. Armah
5. Ngugi					5. Clark
6. Ekwensi					6.Tutuola
7. Okigbo					7. Ekwensi
8. Abrahams					8. Okigbo
9. Okara					9. Okot
10. Armah					10. Mphahlele
11. Mphahlele					11. Abrahams
12. Okot					12.Brutus
13. Brutus					13. Okara
14. Awoonor					14. La Guma
15. La Guma					15. Awoonor
16. Nzekwu					16. Head
17. Aluko					17. Rotimi
18. Liyong					18. Emecheta

Table Three graphically reveals fluctuations over time in the relative standing of the top eighteen writers, with some moving up the scale (e.g., Ngugi, Okot, La Guma), others moving down (Tutuola, Okigbo, Abrahams, Okara), still others holding steady (Soyinka, Achebe, and more recently, Armah), and a fourth unstable group bouncing up and down or down and up (Mphahlele, Awoonor, Clark). Again, the grand weighted total shows us the final resting place of each writer as of the end of 1986.

TABLE FOUR

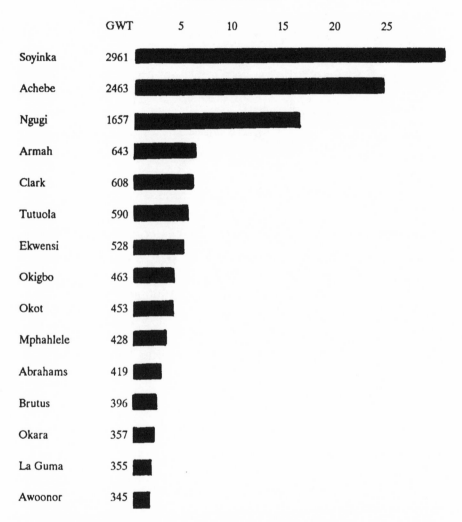

	GWT	5	10	15	20	25
Soyinka	2961					
Achebe	2463					
Ngugi	1657					
Armah	643					
Clark	608					
Tutuola	590					
Ekwensi	528					
Okigbo	463					
Okot	453					
Mphahlele	428					
Abrahams	419					
Brutus	396					
Okara	357					
La Guma	355					
Awoonor	345					

Table Four gives us a graphic illustration of the commanding lead achieved by the front-running troika (Soyinka, Achebe, Ngugi). Certainly these three are not likely to be overtaken any time soon; in fact, at each five-year interval so far, they have improved the distance between themselves and the large pack of fellow scribblers they have left behind. Perhaps it would be more appropriate to call them a triumvirate rather than a troika. There can be no doubt that they have already been impressively canonized by the king-makers of African literature—that is, by scholars and critics who publish opinions on literature.

The second measuring instrument I devised, the Better Ultimate Rating Plan, sought to count and calibrate the frequency with which African authors were taught in literature and drama courses at anglophone African universities. In this survey the underlying assumption was that the real king-makers of African literature were not publishing writers and critics but practicing teachers who each term of every year had to assign texts for their students to read. When they taught African literature, which authors and which texts by these authors did the pedagogues prescribe? In other words, what was the teaching canon? After collecting data from reading lists for 194 courses taught at 30 universities in 14 anglophone African nations, it was possible not just to identify the most frequently taught authors but also to specify with some accuracy precisely which of their texts were most consistently selected for classroom use. There is no need to describe the results of the Better Ultimate Rating Plan here (see the preceding chapter for details), but I am calling your attention to one more chart to illustrate the disparities between the preferences of the critics and the preferences of the teachers.

TABLE FIVE

FAMOUS AUTHORS' REPUTATION TEST	BETTER ULTIMATE RATING PLAN	COMBINED RANKINGS
1. Soyinka 2961	1. Soyinka 277	1. Soyinka 2
2. Achebe 2463	2. Ngugi 228	2. Achebe 5
3. Ngugi 1657	3. Achebe 167	Ngugi 5
4. Armah 643	4. Armah 111	4. Armah 8
5. Clark 608	5. Clark 109	5. Clark 10
6. Tutuola 590	6. Okot 107	6. Okot 15
7. Ekwensi 528	7. La Guma 90	7. Okigbo 18
8. Okigbo 463	8. Abrahams 67	8. Abrahams 19
9. Okot 453	9. Brutus 66	9. Brutus 21
10. Mphahlele 428	10. Okigbo 65	La Guma 21
11. Abrahams 419	11. Aidoo 64	11. Okara 26
12. Brutus 396	12. Rotimi 59	Mphahlele 26
13. Okara 357	13. Okara 57	13. Awoonor 29
14. La Guma 355	14. Awoonor 52	Rotimi 29
15. Awoonor 345	15. Githae-Mugo* 45	15. Aidoo 30
16. Head 295	16. Mphahlele 42	16. Tutuola 36
17. Rotimi 266	Sutherland 42	17. Ekwensi 40
18. Emecheta 234	18. Mwangi 37	Head 40
19. Aidoo 229	19. Ngugi wa Mirii* 35	19. Amadi 41
20. Amadi 181	Osofisan 35	20. Osofisan 45
21. Aluko 174	21. Amadi 33	21. Emecheta 49
22. Liyong 171	Peters 33	22. Sutherland 50
23. Farah 156	23. Okpewho 32	23. Peters 51
24. Nwapa 151	24. Head 31	24. Mwangi 54
25. Equiano 147	25. Nkosi 27	25. Mtshali 57
26. Osofisan 138	26. Mtshali 26	26. Nkosi 62
27. Omotoso 133	Kunene 26	
28. Plaatje 127	28. Angira 25	
29. Ogot 126	Marechera 25	
30. Peters 125	30. Tutuola 23	
31. Mtshali 121	31. Serumaga 21	
32. Nzekwu 113	Emecheta 21	
33. Munonye 106	33. Ntiru 17	
34. Mazrui 105	Ekwensi 17	
Sutherland 105		
36. Mwangi 104		
37. Nkosi 101		

*Co-author with Ngugi wa Thiong'o

Comparison of the two lists makes it plain that critics are significantly more interested in Tutuola, Ekwensi, Mphahlele, Head, and Emecheta than teachers are, and that teachers are significantly more interested in La Guma, Aidoo, Rotimi, Sutherland, and Mwangi than critics are. The chart also reveals that critics and teachers are about equally interested in Soyinka, Achebe, Ngugi, Armah, Clark, and Okara.

If we give critics and teachers equal say in determining the canonical figures in contemporary anglophone African literature, what do we find? The Combined Rankings column attempts to settle that question simply by adding the number of an author's position in one list with the number of his or her position in the other, the sum total being an indicator of his or her rightful place in the ultimate order of things at the end of 1986. Perhaps this double-barreled canon is a more reliable guide to literary fame and reputation than either of the single-barreled canons can pretend to be. We must accommodate the views of both the critics and the teachers in order to arrive at a closer approximation to the truth, the whole truth, and nothing but the truth when seeking to pin down something as notoriously slippery as subjective qualitative discriminations.

And of course we have not yet considered another equally important set of figures—namely, sales figures. Which books do readers buy voluntarily simply to read for pleasure? If we subtract from consideration those books read primarily to win academic promotions (the critics' list) as well as those read solely to pass academic examinations (the teachers' list), what do we have left? Which books can hold their own in an open marketplace ruled not by captive readers but by captivated readers? In short, what is the popular canon? I haven't yet devised a sophisticated econometric instrument equal to the task of making such measurements, but I believe it would be interesting to attempt to do so, if only to observe toward what conclusions the quantification of commercial data would drive us.

Of course, the problem of determining popularity might be settled once and for all if we could only hit upon a sure-fire method of compiling an all-time Best Sellers' List. But this kind of high-stakes accounting work requires better book-keeping records than currently are available for public inspection in the African book trade. Most publishers have a natural inclination to exaggerate their successes; they tend to sing a different tune entirely when the day arrives for them to pay royalties to their authors. Firm, clean data might be hard to come by in so spongy a fiscal swamp.

But before we venture too far into such murky realms of pure speculation, let us return to our tidy columns of empirical data and see what brilliant conclusions about canon formation they are able to support. Based on the evidence now before us, what advice can we offer to young writers who may aspire to canonical status, hoping to win their own secure place in the sun? If we look only at the twenty-six names in the combined rankings column and try to isolate their common characteristics, there are several clear patterns that emerge.

1. To be a successful writer, it helps to be a West African, preferably a Nigerian, but there is no great disadvantage to being a Ghanaian. This may only bear out the demographic fact that there are more people living in West Africa than in other parts of the continent, and hence there are more schools, more universities, more general readers, and more public discussion of literature than is the case elsewhere. However, if you cannot be a West African, the next best alternative is to be a South African, but in that event your chances of establishing a reputation will be improved if you live in exile rather than at home. It is not necessarily an insurmountable handicap to be an East African (Ngugi and Okot have done quite well for themselves after all), but the odds seem to be stacked against Central Africans, not one of whom has yet attained any visibility in the anglophone African literary canon.

2. To be a successful writer, it helps to publish your works with a multinational firm rather than with a local publisher who has no means of international distribution. A number of well-known African writers have published some of their books at home, but they tend to have made their greatest impact with the books they have published with Heinemann, Oxford University Press, Longman, or other big British multinational publishers that have offices spread throughout much of anglophone Africa. Femi Osofisan may be the only writer in the top twenty-six who has made a substantial name for himself by publishing the great majority of his works locally, but it is doubtful that he would have done so well in the rankings had he been Tanzanian, Malawian, Zambian or Zimbabwean and adopted the same policy. Fortunately, he, like the rest of his countrymen, has been able to draw upon a huge reading market in Nigeria, where he is a very visible and dynamic force on the national literary scene. The South Africans on the list also would not have had much of an opportunity to get ahead had they not been published by big houses abroad; some of them have seen all their books banned in South Africa.

3. To be a successful writer, it helps if you write something that is acceptable for use in educational institutions. If your book gets adopted as a required text on a nationwide secondary school leaving exam, your fame and possibly your fortune will be assured. Primary school textbooks will do even better financially; with them your fortune will be made but your reputation will not always be enhanced. If for some reason you find it impossible to write for these big markets, the next best thing would be to try to win over the university crowd, but this is a much trickier feat to bring off and far less remunerative. If you succeed, you may score high in reputation, but your royalties could remain meager unless you somehow manage to tap into foreign university markets as well. A large international university readership is the

summmum bonum, probably better than any pension and possibly the only direct means of entry into the canon.

4. To be a successful writer, it helps if you write well. From the evidence before us, it does not seem to matter much which literary form you use or what you choose to write about so long as you express yourself in an interesting manner. You must write so that people will want to read and reread what you have written. Craft is as important as inspiration. Indeed, excellent writing is the only valid passport to literary canonization. With it, one can go far. Without it, a writer will get nowhere.

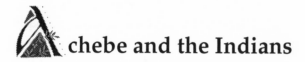chebe and the Indians

From September through mid-December of 1989 I conducted research in India on the teaching of non-British literatures in English departments at Indian universities. I was curious to know to what extent the so-called "new literatures in English" were being taught and studied—not just Third World anglophone literatures from Africa, the Caribbean, and South Asia (most notably from India itself), but also the not-so-new First World literatures from Canada, Australia, New Zealand, and even the United States of America. To put it another way, I wanted to find out how far university English studies in India, a former British colony, had been decolonized since independence. How much of the rest of the English-speaking world was now visible in the literature curriculum? Which authors and which texts from outside the traditional English canon were being read? And how seriously were they being studied? Did the courses in which they were covered make up part of the program of work required of all undergraduate and postgraduate students, or were such courses relegated to the status of exotic options available to whomever might wish to venture a bit beyond the mainstream syllabus? Did non-British literatures command as much respect in Indian universities as British literature?

I had done a similar survey of curricular change in anglophone Africa three years earlier, examining the degree to which African literature had been accommodated in English programs at 40 universities in 14 independent nations. The results of that study showed that African literature was being taught on nearly all the campuses surveyed (the University of Mauritius being the only exception), and that in a few places it had achieved paramountcy, figuring in fifty percent or more of the courses required for a literature degree. In most undergraduate programs, however, British literature still got the lion's share of attention. North American literature, especially its African-American and Afro-Caribbean offshoots, had made striking gains here and there, but the literary output of the remainder of the English-speaking world (India, Canada, Australia, New Zealand, Singapore, and the South Pacific islands) had been granted almost no recognition at all, being virtually ignored in even the most innovative programs. The tendency was for African and other black literatures to drive out some of the British literature but never to rout it completely. Many English departments claimed to be aiming at a balanced curriculum, one that exposed students to the classic British authors (Shakespeare, Dickens, and the rest) as well as to the best contemporary African writers, but there was little agreement on what constituted the ideal mix. One program's balance was another program's disequilibrium. The winds of curricular change were still blowing across the African continent, so the dust hadn't quite settled yet.

In India, on the other hand, the opening up of the English curriculum to non-British subject matter had been a slower and more orderly process. It had proceeded in three distinct phases, with American literature, aided by a postwar infusion of Fulbright funds for teaching and research, infiltrating the syllabus in a significant way in the 1950s, then Indian literature in English gaining a secure academic foothold about a decade later, and finally "Commonwealth Literature" (by which was meant the literatures of the rest of the English-speaking world) earning a small niche for itself only as recently as the 1970s and 1980s. But not all English programs in the nation were affected by these changes in the same way. Today there are still some English departments at Indian universities that teach only British literature, others that teach mainly British literature with a small admixture of American and Indian literatures, and yet others that offer courses in American, Indian, and Commonwealth literatures only at the postgraduate level. In fact, the great majority of English programs at Indian universities remain steadfastly anglocentric, elevating British literature above all others and tolerating little substantive deviation from the type of curriculum that existed during colonial times. Some of these fossilized programs appear to have resisted or effectively deflected the winds of change. Unlike their counterparts in anglophone Africa, most university English departments in India have not undergone a major curricular revolution. Britannia still rules the syllabus.

But in those institutions where there has been change, that change has been broader and more truly international than in Africa. This larger vision is reflected in other ways as well. For instance, there is so lively an interest in Australian literature in India today that an *Indian Journal of Australian Studies* has been launched. There are also at least half a dozen journals devoted almost entirely to Commonwealth literature, three of which—*The Literary Criterion*, *The Literary Half-Yearly*, and *Commonwealth Quarterly*—have been published in one city (Mysore in south India) for an average of twenty years or more. Academic conferences are held periodically on African, Caribbean, Canadian, Australian, and New Zealand literatures as well as on Commonwealth literature, and professional scholarly bodies have sprung up to cater to the interests of researchers specializing in one or more of these new literatures in English. In addition, American literature has continued to receive a great deal of serious scholarly attention, and Indian literature in English has gradually emerged as a major new literary discipline in the Indian academic world. In short, in those places in India where curricular or extracurricular innovation has occurred, there has been a noticeably greater literary cosmopolitanism than in Africa. Indian scholars interested in the wider world of English studies tend to look outward as much as they look inward; they are not entirely preoccupied with local matters.

Of course, such cosmopolitanism can have its hazards. It is difficult for any individual, no matter how industrious, to gain a thorough mastery of half a dozen national literatures and of the distinctive cultures from which they have emerged. This difficulty is compounded when, as in India, there is a serious shortage of primary and secondary texts published abroad. A scholar with limited access to such vital resources is not likely to become an authority in his field, especially if that field consists of several large subplots widely separated in time and space and forever in need of attentive cultivation. By attempting to stretch himself thin over such distant territories and to work without adequate tools, the Commonwealth literature scholar in India runs the risk of becoming a jack of all anglophone literatures and a master of none.

But despite such obstacles, despite such hazards, there exists among the most broadminded of Indian scholars a lively curiosity about new literary phenomena elsewhere and a readiness to move circumspectly into Third World regions where orthodox Anglophiles fear to tread. A little knowledge may be a dangerous thing, but it can also be a delightful thing, leading to insights that otherwise might never occur to a mind devoid of such knowledge. A number of adventurous Indian scholars have been willing to take the risks attendant upon exploring unfamiliar African literary landscapes, and their gambles have paid off not only for themselves but also for others who have been exposed to the new ideas these scholars have generated and disseminated. By venturing rather far afield, they have made fresh discoveries that have helped to draw India and Africa much closer together intellectually.

Before looking at a few examples of their work, it may be well to say a few words about how African literature is taught at Indian universities, for the demands of teaching may influence or even determine the supply of scholarship in a given area, especially a brand-new area. In India, African literature usually is taught as a component in courses on Commonwealth literature. Out of 66 Indian university English departments that responded to a questionnaire sent to 110 institutions eliciting information about current teaching practices, only three reported offering a separate course on African literature, and in one of these, the coverage of Africa was combined with coverage of literature from the West Indies. A few departments taught representative African texts in courses on "Post-colonial Literature," "The New Literatures in English," and "Modern Fiction," but the large majority (25 of the 33 that fielded such new courses) subsumed African literature under the umbrella of "Commonwealth Literature." One practical consequence of this absorption was that only a few African works were being read in these courses—usually two or three at the most, but sometimes merely a single text. Judging from the sample of responses received, one could conclude that half (i.e., 33 of the 66 respondents) of the university English departments in India now offer at least one course on the new literatures in English but that the African component of such courses is quite small, though perhaps no smaller than that of any other area of the Commonwealth.

What does an Indian teacher of a course on Commonwealth literature do when confronted with the problem of selecting one or two texts to represent the literary output of the entire African continent? From the evidence now in hand, the answer is clear: teach Achebe. If there is extra time, teach Soyinka too and then perhaps Ngugi and a few poets, but start with the most important writer and the most significant single text. Start with Achebe. Start with *Things Fall Apart*. Achebe's works were taught in 37 courses at 32 of the 33 institutions in Africa that reported offering courses in the new literatures in English. *Things Fall Apart* was the text selected in 24 of these courses, *Arrow of God* and *No Longer at Ease* were chosen in 3 courses each, *A Man of the People* was used in 2 courses, and selections from Achebe's poetry and short stories were assigned in 3 courses.

In comparison, Soyinka's works were required reading in 28 courses at 25 institutions, but there was no consensus on which of his works was most important. *The Road* was used in 11 courses, *A Dance of the Forests* in 6, *The Lion and the Jewel* in 3, and *The Interpreters*, *Kongi's Harvest*, and *Death and the King's Horseman* in 2 each. Ngugi's works were assigned in only 10 courses at 9 institutions: *Homecoming* and *A Grain of Wheat* in 2 courses each, and *The River Between, Weep Not, Child, Devil on the Cross*, and *Decolonizing the Mind* in one course each. Other authors occasionally read in Indian university English courses included Okigbo and Okara in 3 courses each, Armah and Clark in 2 each, and Awoonor, Brutus, Coetzee, Gordimer, La Guma, Paton, Peters, and Rubadiri in one each. These statistics prove very clearly that Achebe is the African author most frequently taught and that *Things Fall Apart* is the African text most widely read at these institutions. Most Indian students are introduced to African literature through Achebe, and for some of them African literature begins and ends with *Things Fall Apart*.

The same pattern holds in Indian scholarship on African literature. Although there have been occasional essays covering such writers as Abrahams, Amadi, Brutus, Clark, Egbuna, Mphahlele, Mwangi, Nwankwo, Nwapa, Okara, Okigbo, p'Bitek, Rubadiri, Ruganda, and Tutuola, most attention has been focused on the big three: Achebe, Soyinka, and to a far lesser extent, Ngugi. Moreover, the interest in Soyinka and Ngugi is relatively recent, but discussion of Achebe's work goes back a full quarter of a century. Again, the bulk of the commentary on Achebe has dealt with *Things Fall Apart*, the book Indian teachers and students know best.

Indian scholars have adopted a variety of approaches to Achebe's writing. One favorite tactic is to compare his themes and techniques to those employed by writers from India and other Third World countries. Ahmed Ali, R.K. Narayan, Raja Rao, Mulk Raj Anand, Kamala Markandaya, V.S. Naipaul, George Lamming and Gabriel García Marquez have been singled out for comparisons of this kind. So have certain African and African-American writers, namely Cyprian Ekwensi, T.M. Aluko, Ngugi wa Thiong'o, Richard Wright, Ralph Ellison, and James Baldwin. The comparative approach has the double advantage of setting Achebe's achievements in a larger context of literary creativity and simultaneously providing a sufficiently limited number of points of reference for meaningful indepth analysis. The critic can thus study Achebe both from a distance and close up by rubbing him against his peers and observing where the side-by-side contacts yield the greatest sparks of insight. The results sometimes can be quite illuminating.

Another variety of scholarship favored by Indian academics is close reading of the sort commonly referred to as "New Criticism." This approach, no longer new, focuses on the text alone, exploring aspects of its texture and avoiding any examination of its social and political context. This is a safe mode of entry into African literature for readers who have never been to Africa and therefore cannot speak with any confidence about the particular environment out of which a work has emerged. By concentrating on the word rather than on the world behind the work, they can attempt to come to terms with aesthetic dimensions of a literary text. They are concerned almost exclusively with verbal artistry.

A third approach adopted by Indian scholars who write about Achebe is a kind of thematic explication that deals primarily with the subjects, issues, and ideas that animate Achebe's writing. In such criticism, the background of the author or a text may be foregrounded to explain the situation or predicament in real life that appears to have inspired the literary work. Here biographical, historical, sociological, or economic factors may play a significant role in the analysis, but sometimes these contextualizing phenomena may be extrapolated or intuited from the text rather than from a close investigation of the life and times of the author. For instance, one can easily deduce from internal evidence alone that in his fiction Achebe seeks to locate where the rain began to beat his people; a critic would not necessarily have to consult textbooks on colonial history or meteorology to confirm that such precipitation actually occurred. The novels themselves offer convincing evidence of heavy weather and of Achebe's effort to understand and record the damage done during an unusually long tropical rainy season.

Of course, in India, as in other parts of the world where Achebe's works are discussed, different interpretations of the same literary data do arise. There has been at least one good academic fistfight in Indian journals concerning the significance in *Things Fall Apart* of the death of Okoli, a minor character in the Christian community in Mbanta who is alleged to have killed the sacred python (see the articles by Dipak Pal and Bala Kothandaraman). The vigor and persuasiveness of argumentation in this debate reveal an intelligent attentiveness to the text that bodes well for African literature studies in India. If nothing else, it shows that critics there do care about what they read and sometimes care passionately enough to quarrel about subtle points of interpretation. And this is done in classic contestatory style, an energetic mode of debate sufficiently blunt and forceful to undercut the common notion of Indians as a nonviolent people!

In fact, there is nothing in Indian criticism of Achebe and his works that sets it apart from criticism being done elsewhere. Indian critics have been drawn to formal and contextual issues just as critics in other parts of the world have been. They have also made productive use of whatever secondary sources they have found available, though their range of reference, particularly to journals and books published in Africa, may not be as wide as that of scholars who have access to fuller university libraries. Nonetheless, they are quite serious about what they do, and their appraisals of matters that touch close to home—topics such as Achebe's handling of colonialism, nationalism, ethnicity, religion, culture conflict, and stylistic innovation in a second language— frequently are insightful and well-informed. They bring another Third World perspective to bear on Achebe's works, a perspective shaped to some degree by a similar Third World historical and cross-cultural experience. In certain important ways they are closer to their subject than European and American critics are.

There are also a few Indian critics who operate from a base outside India—some of them (such as Uma Parameswaran in Canada, P.D. Tripathi in Zambia, and Eira Patnaik in the United States of America) temporarily or permanently teaching abroad, others (such as Abdul JanMohamed, Peter Nazareth, and Bahadur Tejani, all of whom are East African Asians by origin) having migrated from one location in the Indian diaspora to another (JanMohamed and Nazareth to the USA, Tejani to Nigeria and then to the USA). These peripatetic scholars have increased international awareness of Achebe's writing by publishing articles and books in whatever part of the world they happen to inhabit. JanMohamed's commentaries are particularly noteworthy as sophisticated contributions to contemporary literary theory; his *Manichean Aesthetics* is one of the best theoretical works written on African literature.

Another group of scholars who should not be ignored in this survey are the translators. Translations of samples of Achebe's writing have appeared in at least six Indian languages. *Things Fall Apart* has been published in its entirety in Panjabi and Sinhalese; *No Longer at Ease* is also available in book form in Sinhalese, and *A Man of the People* was serialized in a daily newspaper in this language, which is spoken primarily in Sri Lanka; extracts from Achebe's poetry and criticism have been anthologized in Tamil; an extract from his fiction has been anthologized in Bengali; several of his short stories have appeared in Hindi journals and newspapers; and one cultural magazine called *Pustaka Prapancha*, which is published in the Kannada language, has devoted an entire issue to commentary on and translations of examples of Achebe's work. I doubt that any other African author has been made available to the South Asian reading public in so many Indian languages. To top it all off, there is a separate English edition of *Things Fall Apart* published and distributed locally by Allied Publishers, which has branch offices in eight of India's largest cities.

Why is Achebe so popular in India? I suspect it is for much the same reason that he is popular elsewhere: his books are a pleasure—a very deep pleasure—to read. As one Indian critic put it when commenting on Achebe's first novel,

> *Things Fall Apart* appears to have been able to cast its spell on readers all the world over principally because of Achebe's seemingly artless but really dexterous handling of a theme which

> is essentially local and limited in nature but assumes perennial
> relevance and universal significance (Gupta 55).

"Seemingly artless," "really dexterous," "essentially local and limited in nature" but also "perennially relevant and universally significant"—these are qualities characteristic of a classic work of art, qualities bearing the indelible signature of a master craftsman. Because Achebe's works have been able to "cast their spell on readers all the world over" for more than thirty years, he has gained recognition, in India and elsewhere, as Africa's leading literary guru, an enchanter and sage whose words carry extra weight. And because his popular following continues to grow year by year, he will surely remain a guru—perhaps India's only African guru—for many years to come.

The Writer as Teacher

D.O. Fagunwa as an Educator

Autobiographical writing has already emerged as a distinctive genre in African literature. Indeed, there are so many examples of self-revelation available today that it is possible to sort them into convenient categories and examine each group collectively and comparatively as characteristic responses to a particular kind of African experience. For instance, one could study the nostalgic childhood reminiscences of eminent authors (Laye, Abrahams, Soyinka), the political memoirs of famous politicians (Nkrumah, Mboya, Awolowo, Kaunda), the prison diaries of ex-detainees (Soyinka, Ngugi, Kariuki), the wartime journals of soldiers (Obasanjo, Amadi, Madiebo), the political complaints of South African exiles (Mphahlele, Hutchinson, Modisane, Matshikiza, Nkosi, Mokgatle), the thick ethnographic descriptions of men and women of two worlds (Kenyatta, Gatheru, Okafor-Omali, Waciuma), the travel narratives of adventurers (Ajala, Mukasa, Equiano), the heroic struggles of students overseas (Kayira, Egbuna, Ajao, Onyeama, Clark), the true confessions of rogues and prostitutes (Boetie, Mote). A field so broad covers a lot of interesting territory.

One can also find in some African novels, plays, and poems discernible traces of autobiographical content, intriguing hints that tempt literary critics to trespass on private terrain when making their own interpretations public. But anyone who has tried to distinguish fact from fabrication in autobiographical fiction—or, for that matter, in fictionalized autobiography—will know how slippery this ground can be even for the sure-footed and how frequently such speculative explorations lead to dead ends. Since autobiography never tells the whole truth and nothing but the truth, criticism built on it cannot pretend to be an exact science. The best we can do is to look for suggestive correspondences that illuminate some murky corner of an author's creative imagination. We must content ourselves with probabilities rather than certainties.

One place where autobiography can be genuinely helpful is in literary biography, but for some reason few literary biographies of African authors have been attempted. Perhaps it is too early to expect them, for most major African writers are still alive and kicking, and would-be biographers may prefer to remain outside the range of their kicks. The illustrious dead authors present daunting problems of another sort, mainly due to a lack of adequate sources of biographical data (e.g., letters, unpublished manuscripts, official personal documents, newspaper cuttings, tape recordings, films, etc.) on which a factual reconstruction of a life could be based. Until African libraries begin collecting such materials, scholars will have no chance to write authoritative literary biographies. Indeed, the earliest generation of African writers may well become forgotten men and women if this archival deficiency is not remedied soon. Fifty or one hundred years from now it may be impossible to collect their literary remains.

But in the meantime we should proceed to make use of whatever biographical fragments are within our reach. Some of these—for instance, recently published autobiographical books—are easy to obtain. Other important bits of information are buried in serial and ephemeral publications that have long been out of print. I shall examine here a few items gleaned from obscure Nigerian magazines to see what they can tell us about the life and works of the late Daniel Olorunfemi Fagunwa.

First, a few elementary facts. We know that Fagunwa was born at Okè-Igbó in Western Nigeria in 1903 (Bamgbose 1). After completing eight years in primary school (1916-1924) and three more years in teacher training (1926-1929), he spent ten years as a teacher and principal of the nursery section of St. Andrew's Practising School in Oyo (1930-1939). Instruction at this mission school would have been in Yoruba, his mother tongue, and it was not long before Fagunwa started writing materials in Yoruba that could be used in primary school classrooms. In 1936 he entered his first long narrative, *Ogbójú Ode nínú Igbó Irúnmalè* (The Hunter in the Forest of the Four Hundred Daemons, subsequently translated by Wole Soyinka under the title *The Forest of a Thousand Daemons*), in a competition sponsored by the Church Missionary Society, which promptly bought the manuscript and published it in 1938. This book became very popular as a school reader and has never since gone out of print. He went on to write four more long narratives, two travel books, a collection of stories, and a series of graded primary school readers. By 1965 it was estimated that the total printing of his six major works ran into hundreds of thousands of copies (Beier 51), making him, next to Achebe, the most widely read African author not just in Nigeria but possibly—at least statistically—in the whole of the African continent. (For further biographical details see Bamgbose.)

His narratives are folkloric adventure tales that appeal to adults as well as to children. A Yoruba scholar summarized a typical plot by Fagunwa as follows:

> One fine day, a brave hunter finds his way into a thick jungle in search of big game. He encounters the most fearful monsters, fights with a giant snake with a human head and wrestles with a ghost with one eye in front and one eye at the back of his head. Armed with his gun, the charms of his forefathers and an unshakable belief in an omnipotent God, he comes out successfully in all these encounters. On returning home, he is appointed by the chief of his town to lead a group of men to a far-off land in search of wisdom. They miss their way into the outskirts of hell and wander through curious places like the city of dirt where nobody has ever thought of the idea of having a bath and the city where all the inhabitants eat, drink, laugh or weep simultaneously. After more trouble and hair-breadth escapes, they reach their goal and return home richer and wiser. (Olubummo 26)

As can be seen from this synopsis, Fagunwa blends motifs from traditional Yoruba hunters' tales with a number of Christian notions to achieve a syncretic episodic narrative. He invariably ends his stories with moral advice for his audience.

In 1935-36, possibly while working on his first long narrative, Fagunwa published two brief articles in *The Nigerian Teacher* on "What the School Can Do," describing a strategy for community education he had adopted at St. Andrew's a few years earlier. In the opening paragraph he stated the crux of the problem confronting his school.

> For many years our buildings have been spacious, our staff has been strong, our manager has been of the keenest type, and our school equipment has been ample. But despite all these attractions the people of the district would not send in their children and the attendance was small. In the latter part of 1933 our children numbered only a little over forty, and most of these were in danger of being withdrawn for this or that reason, mostly for financial difficulties. In fact, those that could be regarded as reliable members of the school scarcely numbered above thirty. It became imperative that something should be done to prevent this steady decrease in the numbers of the school....It became necessary, therefore, that the school should try to impress its achievements upon the district. (46)

The tactic chosen to make this impression was a visit by the school children to a local marketplace. Special songs were composed for the occasion, some of the children were assembled into a percussion band, and the whole group marched to the market carrying books, pencils, and papers. Their singing and drumming immediately attracted a large crowd, who listened attentively to a series of brief speeches and readings by the students and watched a demonstration of the students' writing skills. Fagunwa himself then gave a short concluding oration, and the children, with more songs and music, marched triumphantly back to school, followed by many enthusiastic villagers. A few months later the children made a second expedition to the compound of a local chief. This time they gave demonstrations not only of their academic abilities but also of their gardening skills and knowledge of first aid. The program ended with a display of dancing and storytelling by the youngest children at the school, girls aged two and three.

As a result of these extremely successful public relations efforts, enrollment in the school doubled the following year. Fagunwa closed his essay by drawing an appropriate moral.

> I think this is the kind of thing that Nigeria needs, especially at the present moment. From the statistics of the Government it will be found that only a small minority of our children receive school education, and even many of the children of our chiefs are not included in this minority....We as teachers need to interest parents in the work of the school, bearing in mind that a society is not being improved when the units of which it is composed are not being developed. (48)

It is obvious that Fagunwa's tactics as an educator were quite similar to those he employed as a storyteller. Believing in the educational value of good entertainment, he attempted to amuse and instruct at the same time. He deliberately shaped his art— be it a story, an essay, a speech, or a dramatic display—so that it would lead to a fitting moral. Delight was the means by which he sought to achieve his didactic ends.

The clearest articulation of Fagunwa's credo as an artist appears in an article he published in another Nigerian teachers' magazine twenty-five years later. By this time he was well-known as an author, educator, civil servant, and publisher's representative, for after holding various teaching and administrative posts in schools, he had worked as an Education Officer with the Publications Branch of the Ministry of Education in Western Nigeria for five years and then as Nigerian representative for Heinemann Educational Books. He had also spent seven years in England studying at the School of Oriental and African Studies at the University of London. All but one of his major works had been published by 1960, the year his essay on "Writing a Novel" was printed in a Ministry of Education journal called *Teachers' Monthly*. Here is the entire text of this interesting document.

Teachers often ask questions on the writing of a novel. Of late these questions have increased. How do novelists produce their works? What is the difference between a publisher and a printer? What are phantasia novels? etc. Here an attempt is made to reply [to] some of these questions, and the reply represents my own personal opinion.

A novel is a written prose fiction. It has developed from the word "romance" which is applicable to verse as well. Also we sometimes hear of "Novels in Verse". In other words the writing of a long story in a connected form, which, though it had not happened, is presented as though it, in fact, had happened, may be regarded as a novel.

The aim of a novelist is to present to the public something interesting to read, and the success or failure of a novel lies in how far it can get hold of its readers and compel them to read on. This is why its place is of special importance in a community such as ours where people as a rule do not read works in their own languages except in so far as they have a bearing on the passing of this or that examination.

Now, all aspects of life do not interest people equally. Love for instance interests most people. We like to love and be loved. We also like to watch those who are loving or being loved. Money interests all: we need at least some for our existence and so we are interested further in the rich and the poor. Adventure interests some but not all. We hear of people who walk long distances, swim wide expanse of water or climb mountains. The mysterious interests us in one way or another. What for instance happens to us after death? Is it true that if we behave well on earth we go to Paradise and otherwise to hell? Are there ghosts? Do spirits inhabit trees, rocks, rivers, streams, etc? What a novelist does is to present one or more of these aspects of life and weave a long story around whichever he takes.

All these aspects of life are not equally difficult to write about. A novel based on love is not very difficult to write because even if all the true stories of love we hear are written and joined, they easily look like fiction. Equally a novel based on money is not very difficult to write since stories connected with misappropriation of money are common in real life.

A novel which involves the mysterious is perhaps the most difficult to write. In such a case, the writer goes really into the world of imagination and therefore it is necessary for him to have had an inborn gift of imagination. In literary history, only few brains had produced this type of writing and the products have lived long.

John Bunyan has been described as the father of English novels. His *Pilgrim's Progress* describes no other thing than the journey from this world to the world to come. So is Spenser's *Faerie Queenne* [sic], a novel in verse.

The term "Phantasia novels" is an invention used for describing novels written in African languages in Nigeria but, in literary language, I have never heard of that term. However, I know the type of novels that the majority of Western Nigerians have written, my having been a long time in the Publication Section of this Ministry, and being responsible for reading and assessing Government publications has placed me in a position to know what our people write about.

Let me say, in the first place that it is not correct to say that all Nigerian novels have something of phantasy in them but the majority do. I usually term these Spenserian because they so much resemble the works of an English writer, whose works were published in the late sixteenth and early seventeenth century A.D., called Edmund Spenser. The fact about them is that if well handled they have a peculiarly forceful way of driving an idea home. They interest Nigerian readers a good deal and I have always encouraged rather than discouraged them. Compare this personification in Book I of Spenser's *Faerie Queenne*. In Spenser's view, the reformed Church was full of misdeeds. He does not as a result describe these acts of omission and commission in mere words, but instead, he personifies Error as a horrible monster half-serpent half-woman living in a dark, filthy cave, to be fought by a knight who himself was the son of a fairy. Here, when everything of the misdeeds of the Church could have been forgotten, the picture of this monster would remain in the mind.

As has been pointed out above, our duty is to present to our readers what we know will interest them. We should not merely copy others but should give first consideration to the need of our society. Experience has shown that British humour is not the same as the African's, and while it is doubtful whether the British would like an element of phantasy in a novel, surely some of the continentals will do. Besides, there is nothing wrong in making our own kind of writing our special contribution to the literary history of the world. Nigerian society is broadly divided into two, namely, the educated section and the non-educated, (those who had been to school and those who have never been). A big slice of the former together with nearly all the latter believe in juju, spirits, ghosts, etc., and a novelist should take an account of this. (12)

It is worth noting that Fagunwa puts his emphasis on invention, not on style. In fact, hardly a word is said about the manner in which an author ought to express himself. Fagunwa evidently placed matter before manner, subject before style, in his literary scale of values. He knew that every novelist aspires "to present to the public something interesting to read," but he felt that the best way for any writer to attempt to fulfill this aspiration was through careful selection of a theme that would have widespread popular appeal. Money and love were not only intrinsically interesting subjects but were also quite easy to write about because everyone knew something about them from firsthand experience. Adventure stories, on the other hand, did not have universal appeal but were of interest to some readers. The kind of fiction that fascinated people "in one way or another" but was "perhaps the most difficult to write" because it required "an inborn gift of imagination" was the kind that Fagunwa himself most favored and always wrote—a kind known then in Western Nigeria as the "Phantasia novel."

As its name implied, the Phantasia novel contained elements of fantasy derived from the "world of imagination." It was not rooted in tangible, mundane realities but was concerned with "the mysterious"—that is, with otherworldly notions that could not be verified empirically. Notice that Fagunwa defines "the mysterious" as a realm of metaphysical speculation. He is not interested in writing whodunits, gothic romances, or science fiction. His eye is fixed on the larger mysteries of life and death, flesh and spirit, essence and existence.

> What for instance happens to us after death? Is it true that if we behave well on earth we go to Paradise and otherwise to hell? Are there ghosts? Do spirits inhabit trees, rocks, rivers, streams, etc.? (12)

Fagunwa, Nigeria's foremost Phantasia novelist, was a transcendentalist at heart.

This becomes even clearer when he cites examples of English fiction concerned with "the mysterious." The first work mentioned, John Bunyan's religious allegory *The Pilgrim's Progress*, is not at all surprising because Bunyan has frequently been discussed as an important source of inspiration for Fagunwa. (Bamgbose 24-26, Lindfors 1970) But Spenser's *The Faerie Queene*, an allegorical verse epic antedating *The Pilgrim's Progress* by nearly a century, comes as a mild shock because one does not expect that someone with Fagunwa's fairly limited educational background would have been exposed to this venerable classic. Certainly no literary critic or commentator on Fagunwa's writing has ever mentioned it as being among the books that had an impact on him. Yet, in retrospect, Fagunwa's reference to Spenser seems perfectly natural and right. *The Faerie Queene* displays precisely the kind of vivid didactic transcendentalism that makes both Bunyan's *The Pilgrim's Progress* and Fagunwa's *The Forest of a Thousand Daemons* so memorable. All three are episodic religious parables that imaginatively explore "the mysterious" through allegory. All three attempt to entertain as well as instruct.

Fagunwa evidently felt that literature, even at its most diverting and pleasurable, ought to have a serious purpose. In fact, he considered it the writer's duty to capture the attention of readers and "compel them to read on" for their own edification and enjoyment. If literature did nothing more than to promote greater literacy among people who were unaccustomed to reading outside of school, it would still justify its existence. But a larger purpose would be served if the author could induce the educated and non-educated to ponder some of the big questions of life. This, Fagunwa felt, could be accomplished through adroit use of "phantasy." The underlying motive was not to help readers escape from the realities of life but to lead them to confront the larger spiritual realities in which their lives ultimately were rooted. By making readers think as well as feel, the writer would improve the quality of their intellectual and imaginative experience.

But one couldn't accomplish all this through dull writing. The writer certainly shouldn't bore his audience. This is where his own "inborn gift of imagination" was of such crucial importance. The writer couldn't fulfill his responsibilities to his fellow man if he wrote uninteresting stories or if he borrowed his material from abroad. "We should not merely copy others but should give first consideration to the need of our society." The author, in other words, should write original fiction custom-tailored to suit the aesthetic preferences of Nigerian readers. His matter and his manner should be uncompromisingly African. Only if he achieved this self-confidence and rare creative independence could he make a profound impact on his society. And only then would he stand a chance of earning immortality by "making our own kind of writing our special contribution to the literary history of the world."

Fagunwa's literary philosophy reveals him to be an artist somewhat ahead of his times. In modern parlance we might call him a "committed writer," a "cultural nationalist," or a purveyor of "black consciousness" in literature. At a time when many other African authors were addressing their messages to Europe and experimenting with foreign literary forms and fashions, Fagunwa was intent on speaking to his own people in an imaginative idiom they could understand and appreciate. He affirmed the value of African verbal traditions even while exploring the relevance and utility of imported modes of expressive art. He combined indigenous morality with Christianity, the folktale with allegory and parable, politics and metaphysics with art, creating in the process his own distinctive genre of didactic, transcendental prose fiction. He was Nigeria's first classic storyteller and first modern novelist, and it is unlikely that his narratives will ever be forgotten. Someone ought to write a fullscale literary biography of this important African writer someday soon.

Okot's Last Blast: An Attempt at Curricular Reform in Uganda after Idi Amin

The late Okot p'Bitek, Uganda's most famous singer-poet, is remembered by his friends as a genial maverick who tried to reshape modern East African culture by laughing at its worst excesses. A skilled satirist, he directed his most exuberant attacks at what he termed "apemanship," the educated African's unthinking acceptance of Western ways (*Revolution* 5). Any manifestation of African deference to European customs and traditions—whether it be a teachers' college choir singing "Bobby Shaftoe's Gone to Sea" at celebrations marking Kenya's national day, or Ugandan undergraduates learning Scottish "tribal dances," or African lawyers and judges wearing gowns and wigs and conducting their proceedings in English, or brides and grooms being pelted with rice upon leaving church after getting married—would be singled out by Okot for hilarious ridicule, with all the abundant absurdities attendant upon such eccentric cross-cultural exercises duly noted. Okot had a keen eye for comic incongruity and loved to poke fun at the foibles of his elite contemporaries. As a literary artist he is best-known for a long comic poem, *Song of Lawino* (1966), in which an uneducated Acholi woman laments the peculiar behavior of her highly educated husband who has become so thoroughly Westernized that he despises everything African, even his own skin and hair. Lawino's amusingly ironic litany of marital complaints turned out to be the perfect vehicle for conveying Okot's ideas about African "apemanship."

But underlying Okot's genial satirical humor was a serious political argument that questioned the wisdom of Africa's continued reliance on European cultural institutions, particularly schools and universities built on a foreign model that perpetuated notions of Western cultural superiority. He was extremely critical of university courses in the humanities that dealt entirely with alien subject matter and never paid attention to local examples of the same phenomena. In essays, lectures, and interviews—some of which subsequently were collected in a volume called *Africa's Cultural Revolution* (1973)—he advocated the indigenization of the entire curriculum, even going so far as to suggest that illiterate village singers, dancers, musicians, and carvers be employed by African universities to teach African arts to undergraduates. He believed that

> The cultural revolution in Africa is the revolt against Western cultural domination....The schools and universities of Africa, which until recently were the most powerful institutions for inculcating the totally irrelevant cultural values of the ruling classes of the West, must be shaken up, and challenged to take part in—no, to lead—the cultural revolution that is taking place. (*Revolution* 17)

African education, he argued, should serve African interests, and it can only do so by putting Africa at the heart of the curriculum. This was a nationalist argument, one that sought to liberate African educational institutions and their students from the suffocating stranglehold of neocolonial mind-fetters. Seek ye first the educational kingdom, preached Okot, and all else shall be added unto it.

This was not just empty theorizing in East Africa. The kind of educational revolution Okot envisioned had already been carried out in the English Department at the University of Nairobi, where in September and October of 1968 a group of three young lecturers—Ngugi wa Thiong'o, Henry Owuor-Anyumba, and Taban lo Liyong—formally proposed that the English Department be abolished and replaced with a Department of African Literature and Languages that emphasized the study of indigenous verbal arts, including oral literature. In an official paper spelling out their position, these lecturers stated that

> The aim, in short, should be to orientate ourselves toward placing Kenya, East Africa, and then Africa in the centre [of the curriculum]. All other things are to be considered in their relevance to our situation, and their contribution towards understanding ourselves. (Ngugi wa Thiong'o 146)

European literatures would still be studied for the oblique light they shed on African experience, but in the new syllabus English literature would lose its once-dominant place.

> We see no reason why English literature should have priority over and above other European literatures where we are concerned. The Russian novel of the nineteenth century should and must be taught. Selections from American, German, and other European literatures should also be introduced. In other words English writings will be taught in their European context and only for their relevance to the East African perspective. (Ngugi wa Thiong'o 148)

The successful revolution launched at Nairobi had profound effects on literature teaching in many other parts of anglophone Africa, leading to similar, but usually more limited, experiments in Africanizing the syllabus. Today most English or Literature Departments at anglophone African universities have achieved what they regard as a "balance" between the old colonial curriculum and the new, indigenous postcolonial one, but definitions of what constitutes "balance" differ markedly from one corner of the continent to another. The Nairobi program remains the most radical transformation of literature teaching and literature study anywhere in Africa.

When the Nairobi revolution was set in motion, Okot was not a passive bystander. He had just arrived in Kenya in 1968 to take up an appointment in the Extra-Mural Department at the University of Nairobi, and though he was based much of the time in Kisumu, where he organized arts festivals, he regularly visited Nairobi and kept in close contact with the rebellious lecturers in the English Department, especially with his old friend and former student, Taban lo Liyong. Indeed, Okot provided moral and verbal support to the rebellion, speaking his mind at private strategy sessions and at numerous forums for public debate. For more than a decade in Kenya, as well as at universities in Nigeria and the United States of America where he took up visiting appointments, he remained an articulate advocate of nationalistic literary self-assertion. It is not surprising that he carried these ideas with him when he eventually went home to his motherland.

Okot had left Uganda during the reign of Idi Amin, and he did not return until 1979, shortly after Amin finally was ousted from power. Initially he was absorbed at Makerere University as a Senior Research Fellow in the Institute of Social Research, a post which, according to his son-in-law Lubwa p'Chong, Okot "considered an insult to him, claiming Makerere University, his home university, was dumping him there as a broken lorry....In 1982 the university at last recognized Okot's contribution to the literary world and scholarship and honoured him by appointing him the first professor of creative writing in Makerere, Department of Literature." (p'Chong 9-10).

However, what Okot found in the Department of Literature displeased him. The curriculum had not changed much in the twenty years that had passed since Uganda had become an independent country. A few African writers were studied in special courses on African literature, but the syllabus still emphasized the literature of the British Isles. It was as if the revolution started in Nairobi had completely bypassed Kampala, only a few hundred miles west. Curricular neocolonialism, instead of withering away, remained in full bloom at Makerere.

Indignant, and perhaps a little frustrated by the three-year delay in getting his foot in the door of the department to which he felt he truly belonged, Okot published in the government-owned *Uganda Times* of May 6, 1982, an article entitled "Literature

Department Needs Overhaul" in which he poured scorn on the offerings of the department to which he had just been appointed. Here is the entire text of that document, which may be the last piece of writing by Okot to have been published before his sudden death two and a half months later on July 20, 1982.

There is a grave crisis in the Department of Literature at Makerere.

The final withdrawal of British professors (David Cook and Margaret Macpherson) has been achieved. The entire teaching staff are not merely Africans. They are all Ugandans. But the Department is still one of the whitest of literature departments north of the Cape of Good Hope. The one in the University of Malawi may just beat us in its whiteness in that books by African writers are totally banned.

If you are stupid enough to be found with any of the books of the Malawian poet, novelist, dramatist and former diplomat David Rubadiri, Ngugi wa Thiong'o, one of Africa's foremost novelists, Achebe or Soyinka or my own, you do not only lose your job, but are imprisoned.

The syllabus in the Department of Literature here seems to be deliberately designed to stultify creative talent, and to ensure that the student, after three years of literature will become so thoroughly [fed] up that he or she will think of literature only as torture. But, even more sinister, the syllabus is such that the African student is made to believe that there [are] some literatures, especially those from England and America, which are superior to those of his own people.

The other day Professor Timothy Wangusa reported that poetry was not a popular subject with the students, that it was the worst paper done in the exams. How can poetry, which is the other word for song, be unpopular? A song, a story, a play is enjoyable because it is meaningful. If the poetry that is being offered at Makerere is unpopular, this is precisely because it is meaningless, socially irrelevant to the society from which the student comes. Daffodils! What has this kind of lily, which does not even grow here, mean to us? They plant flowers in Europe at the beginning of a season called Spring, which comes after Winter.

William Shakespeare's works are very interesting. At Makerere there is a whole course devoted to him. There is another course all about American Literature (20 authors). And yet last academic year, Oral Literature was not offered at all. How do we begin to rate Shakespeare, Cooper, Ellison to be superior to Adok Too, the blind poet from Lamogi near Gulu, who was jailed by the British for two years, and was hunted down by Amin's thugs, but was not caught? What of the recitals from Ankole, and the songs of Evaristo Muyinda and Tereza Kisolo at the Museum? What of the story tellers who composed the folk tales? And the wise man and woman who coined the proverbs?

In 1968 a literary revolution overthrew the Department of English at Nairobi University. It was replaced by the Department of Literature with African Literature, both oral and written, as the core of the syllabus. The syllabus did not completely exclude the literatures of other people, but the main emphasis was on African literature. Should African students learn what other artists have done? Of course, but after knowing their own. For only so can they begin to compare what has been produced at home with other people's works. Only so, can our future leaders have firm roots at home, something to be proud about, something they can call their own.

Many of the students who take literature at Makerere are also in the Faculty of Education. When they graduate, whose literature will they teach to the children at secondary schools? Should generosity not begin at home? Thirteen years after, Makerere University's Literature Department is still essentially an English Department. What happened? Why did the revolution in Nairobi fail to reach Makerere? The answer is easy to find.

The European forces there led by the Cooks and Macphersons were still too strong. Pio Zirumu and Nuwa Sentongo and other friends on the Hill were no match. They spent their creative energy, not so much at Makerere, but at the National Theatre where, together with Elvania Zirimu, Robert Serumaga, Byron Kawadwa and many other talents, [they] brought about an unprecedented flowering of Ugandan theatre.

What was the literary revolution in Nairobi all about? Led by Ngugi, Taban, Philip Ochieng, Owuor Anyumba, and myself, we rejected the assumption that Africa should continue to be an extension, an appendage of Europe. We insisted that Africa cannot and should not be interpreted in terms of ideas, and in a vocabulary borrowed from outside. If there is need for the study of the historic continuity of a single culture, why can't it be African? Why and how do you suppose that African culture has its roots in Europe? The other fake notion we refused was the lie that there was something called Universal standards. There is no such thing. What is being paraded before us by that label from Europe is nothing more than the supposed standards of the ruling classes there. What is taught to the children of those fellows is to instil the ideas of the beautiful, etc. And these may not be what we in Uganda and Africa uphold as the beautiful.

For me, culture is philosophy as lived and celebrated in society. Human beings do not behave like dry leaves, smoke or clouds that are blown here and there by the winds. Men live in organizations such as the family, a chiefdom, a nation. He has a religion, an army, legal and many other social institutions. All these organizations are informed by, are built around the central idea of the people, that is, what they believe life is all about.

It is according to a people's social philosophy that human behavior is judged, decent woman, stupid fellow, good boy, brave soldier, thief, etc. Morality and immorality, what is good and what is not good, are measured according to the people's world view. Who is a crook here may be a clever fellow somewhere else. All the creative works of man, literature, painting, sculpture, music and dance, architecture, village and town planning, etc., are all reflections of the philosophy of life of a people. It is the artist who captures and expresses this elusive "thing" called the philosophy of life or world view in his works. He uses his voice, his musical instrument, his body as in the dance or in the theatre, his pen, his gestures, etc., to achieve this. It is the artist who at the same time sustains the moral system by laughing at fools, and praising the good works of members of the society. (5)

Okot's blast at his university department stirred up considerable controversy in Kampala, with some people wondering what could have motivated such a harsh attack. A

BBC correspondent covering the row reported that "It is not known why Professor Okot decided to turn publicly on his own department at this particular time, but there is speculation at Makerere that he may be embarking on a campaign for the job above his own, head of the entire Department of Literature" (Wooldridge 6). While it is not inconceivable that Okot may have had a personal motive for calling for a complete overhaul of his department, the views he expressed are no different from those he articulated earlier in public speeches and published articles. In a previous open letter to Makerere University authorities, he had tried to shift the focus of the cultural debate from individual personalities to institutional policies.

> I insist that there is so much work to be done, none being more difficult than original and creative thinking. Let our professors and lecturers and leaders stop engaging in small and wasteful even childish activities like backbiting others and begin to reflect seriously on the human predicament in this part of the world. For only so can we prevent our university from becoming one huge veneer, a surface refinement hiding the cheapness and sordidness at the heart of things, an institution only fit for the rubbish heap and furnace. (Quoted by p'Chong 10)

This statement is consistent with basic principles Okot had espoused throughout his controversial career: Think big, think creatively, think constructively, but above all, think independently and think African. Do not let small personal vendettas deflect you from nobler national undertakings. Do not waste time engaging in petty academic politics when there are larger issues—jumbo academic politics—that urgently require engagement at a philosophical as well as a practical level. Take pride in indigenous culture: Study it, live it, enjoy it to the full. Resist European cultural domination. Avoid apemanship. Know yourself, be yourself, and be content with yourself.

These are the messages Okot attempted to communicate through all his public activities. As an artist, as an educator, as an agitator, his role was basically the same. He himself was quite conscious of the consistency of his position. In an interview he once said,

> I want to suggest that all my writings, whether they are anthropological monographs, studies of religion, essays, songs, poems, or even traditional stories and proverbs such as I am collecting now, all of them are ammunition for one big battle: the battle to decide where we here in Africa are going and what kind of society we are building. I think you will find great similarities in all the different things I have been producing because they all have basically the same aim. (Lindfors 1980: 143)

So Okot's last blast at Makerere was not a momentary aberration. It was simply another attempt to trumpet a note he had been sounding all his adult life. Unfortunately, the syllabus currently followed in the Literature Department at Makerere exhibits little evidence of having been transformed by the clamor Okot made, but now that he is gone, perhaps the resonant echoes of his voice that linger behind will be heard and heeded. Uganda suffered terrible physical and intellectual devastation during the reign of Idi Amin, but not everyone in the country during that period and after turned stone deaf to Okot's style of singing. He still has a large and appreciative audience fully in tune with his message and eager to help orchestrate Uganda's cultural revolution. If they succeed, Okot will have scored his greatest and most durable hits posthumously.

Disciplinary Concerns

On Disciplining Students in a Non-Discipline

African literature is a specialty rather than a discipline in American universities, and it appears destined to remain so for the foreseeable future. It is an amorphous field offering its devotees neither a large corpus of literary works to study nor established traditions of scholarship to carry on. Indeed, in certain branches of it—particularly the so-called "vernacular literatures"—even the most basic scholarly tools are lacking and responsible research is difficult, if not impossible, to carry out. Until these deficiencies are remedied, African literature is not likely to gain recognition as a separate but equal humanistic discipline in American academia. As scholars we are still too young and unsophisticated to be regarded by our colleagues as peers.

Moreover, our environment is impeding our professional development. Among the extracurricular factors inhibiting the orderly growth of African literature study in the United States are overt and covert racism, widespread ignorance of all things African, shrinking university budgets in a period of high inflation, and deeply-ingrained institutional inertia. In the 1960s, when American cities were burning down and "Black Power" seemed a tangible threat rather than a transitory slogan, universities were quick to respond to demands for Black Studies courses and programs. African literature rode into instant academic respectability on this wave of social turmoil, and many of us who were teaching or earning degrees during these times may actually owe our jobs and subsequent careers to the arsonists, looters, and snipers of Watts, Bedford-Stuyvesant, Hough, and other urban ghettoes. However, as the fiery outbursts of the Johnson years gave way to the ashy intrigues of the Nixon era, the backlash began, and many Black Studies programs found themselves in trouble financially, politically and academically. Today Black Studies programs are often regarded as campus hideouts for anti-intellectual students and professors who lack the ability or inclination to enter more rigorous academic fields. African literature has been tarred with the same brush. It is usually viewed as a nonprofessional, nondescript nondiscipline which only nonentities would consider entering.

One evidence of this ivory tower prejudice is the absence of M.A. and Ph.D. programs in African literature at any American universities other than the University of Wisconsin at Madison and Howard University in Washington, D.C., both of which managed to get their programs started in the 1960s. At other campuses with large African Studies centers—e.g., Northwestern, Indiana, UCLA, Boston, Michigan State—it is still necessary for a student to fulfill all the requirements of one of the orthodox departments (usually English, French, Folklore, or Comparative Literature) before being permitted to write a dissertation on African literature. At campuses without established African Studies centers, the student is likely to discover even greater hurdles placed in his path if he wants to work in what his professors and colleagues perceive as an exotic, dark, lunatic fringe of literary studies. It will be difficult for him to escape being pigeonholed as an oddball, an outsider, a know-nothing, and a short-sighted miscreant who loves his specialty not wisely but too well.

It may also be exceedingly difficult for him to find a job afterwards. The market value of a Ph.D. in African literature has declined just as rapidly as the national interest in Black Studies. Indeed, several of my doctoral students at The University of Texas at Austin have found it much easier to obtain jobs teaching African literature in Africa than in the United States. When interviewed for positions anywhere in North America, they were invariably asked what else they were prepared to teach.

It was virtually impossible for them to find employment teaching only African literature.

Some would say that this is as it should be, and I would agree up to a point. It can be useful and refreshing to teach other subjects, provided one still has an opportunity to grow professionally in one's chosen field. The danger lies in being burdened with so many routine departmental duties that one has no chance to develop any real competence as a scholar or teacher of the literature in which one has been specially trained. The caterpillar forced to spin too many cocoons may well die of exhaustion before he can turn into a butterfly.

What kind of graduate program should be designed for these fragile insects, our graduate students, to help them survive the rigors of a world hostile to their species? What should they be fed and how exercised so as to maximize their chances for healthy growth both before and after receiving their degrees? Given the harsh realities of academic life in the United States today, what is the most practical blueprint for graduate education in African literature?

There can be no simple answer to such questions. Much will depend on the department and institution in which one works; much will depend on the interests and aptitudes of the individual student. It is impossible to outline a uniform program that will satisfy the needs of everyone everywhere now and forevermore. All that most of us can do is to work within the existing structures that others have created for other ends and hope that our efforts will be of some use to somebody. We must remain flexible and adaptable if we—and our students—are to survive.

If we begin with the assumption that most doctoral students of African literature aspire to teach African literature at the college or university level, then our primary responsibility must be to make them fit for employment as teachers of undergraduate and graduate students. Considering the exigencies of the job market today, I think we fail in our mission if we allow or encourage prospective Ph.D.s to specialize exclusively in African literatures. Since it is clear that they must be able to teach something else in order to find an appropriate job, we should make a serious effort to build into their program of study a requirement that they master at least one field outside the domain of African literatures. If their activity in this other field is in some way related to their interest in African literature, that would be well and good, but it should not have to be so related to serve as a viable "minor" concentration. Indeed, since this "minor" may well become the student's major teaching area later on, we should see to it that he receives a sound training in it, even if this takes him away from studies in African literature. To provide him with a real "bread-and-butter" alternative specialty, we must be sure to put teeth into this part of his program.

I am recommending this not as a policy of desperation or as a policy of unconditional surrender to the vagaries of a job market over which we have no control. I do not think we ought to sell out our principles to achieve a better job placement percentage, but I also do not think that we ought to sell our students short. If they must be provided with more skills to be employable, we should give them the opportunity to acquire those skills within the framework of an African literature program. We must change our requirements rather than cripple our students.

I believe that a flexible Ph.D. program that includes a strong "minor"—or, better yet, a double "major"—will benefit not only the student of African literatures but also the study of African literatures. Only when we have scholars who can cut across disciplines and apply approaches to African literatures that they have learned in other fields will our own field truly grow. We ought to do our utmost to encourage this kind of cross-fertilization of ideas and utilization of new and different methodologies. It doesn't matter what other subject the student chooses to study so long as it appears likely to shed some light, however remote or oblique, on some aspect of an African literature. I wouldn't even insist that he work in an adjacent or closely related literary discipline. Illumination often emerges from the most unexpected sources; the only condition required is a strong spark of curiosity.

So let our students go forth and till any field that interests them—Folklore, Linguistics, Music, Art, History, Psychology, Political Science, Library Science, English Literature, French Literature, Portuguese Literature, Papua New Guinea Literature—the list is inexhaustible. And let them master these fields as fully as they master what they are taught about African literatures. Their explorations are likely to enrich us all.

There is only one other requirement I would insist upon in any graduate program designed for advanced study of African literatures. I believe that our graduate students should be taught to write. I do not mean this in the narrow sense of teaching them the rudiments of grammar, spelling, punctuation, and syntax, as one might do in a freshman composition class. Rather, I mean that students preparing to become professional interpreters of African literature should be trained in the methods and techniques of scholarly and critical discourse and should be encouraged to write for publication. I do not think it sufficient for them to address their ideas about African literature only to their professor (as they might, for example, in a term paper) or only to their classmates and professor (as they might in a seminar paper). They should be urged—in fact, forced—to seek a wider audience outside the cozy confines of their immediate university environment. What they write, how they write, or which media they choose to write for is less important than the fact that the do write regularly, that they try as often as possible to communicate their ideas on paper to another group of people elsewhere. Training in the expression and dissemination of ideas should be what graduate education in any field is all about.

The New Racism

There is a new type of racism evident in academia today. Let me give you an example.

One of my doctoral students, a former Peace Corps volunteer, entered the job market this year. On paper he looked fine. Besides having an interesting personal background and university teaching experience in his specialty as well as in most of the standard introductory English courses, he could list an impressive number of publications: a dozen book reviews, half a dozen articles, two pamphlets on contemporary literature, and a dissertation which gave clear signs of growing into his first book. He had completed more than sixty percent of the dissertation by Christmas, and every single chapter had been accepted for publication by a leading journal in his field. His academic record was spotless, his personality pleasant, his hair only moderately long, and his letters of recommendation overflowing with praise from well-known scholars in the United States and Europe. His was the kind of dossier that makes even the best-fed recruitment committees salivate.

He went to the MLA Convention in New York fairly confident of finding a suitable job. He had already spoken with several eager chairmen on the phone and had interviews lined up with thirteen top universities, public and private, large and small, from every part of the country. It seemed only a matter of selecting the most congenial academic and physical environment for beginning his professional career. But his interviewers took one quick look at him and ran away horrified. There were no follow-up phone calls, no invitations to visit the campus, no hard bargaining sessions, no offers, no jobs. All he heard was "I'm sorry, Mr. X, I'm afraid we can offer you no encouragement."

Why? Several interviewers told him quite frankly. Others tried to hint more or less tactfully at what they regarded as his fatal flaw: Mr. X wanted to teach black literature, but unfortunately he had been born white.

This explanation rankled because Mr. X's major area of interest was not African-American literature but African literature, a relatively new field in which it is no special advantage to be African-American (except, apparently, when looking for a university teaching position). A knowledge of Africa is not transmitted genetically; there is absolutely no reason to believe that the great-great-grandson of a slave transported from the Guinea coast 150 years ago will intuitively know more about ancient Yoruba kingdoms, Kikuyu social structure, or the rise and fall of Kwame Nkrumah than will a white or yellow or red American who has spent years studying such things and living in various parts of Africa. To believe otherwise is to be guilty of the grossest racism. Yet this is what many of the best universities in the United States are openly professing today. They admit they would rather hire a totally unqualified black to teach African literature than a well-qualified white.

It was obvious that some departments that interviewed Mr. X did so in the desperate hope that he was black. It was impossible to guess his racial identity from his name, but his teaching experience—two years in Nigeria, one in a black ghetto grade school in New York City—suggested he might be the right shade and hue. "Who else would do such things or want to study such literature?" was probably the official line of reasoning. Mr. X was colorful enough to merit an interview.

But nothing more than an interview, once his academic albinism was discovered. "We are worried about what the Black Students Union would say if we hired you," he was told. "And, of course, HEW might never forgive us." Practical considerations to justify discrimination in reverse. Times change, victims change, but the tactics of prejudicial employers remain pretty much the same. One cautious chairman even took the trouble to phone an old friend on Mr. X's doctoral committee to find out what color he was. He said his department had been very impressed with Mr. X's dossier but they felt they needed information on his pigmentation before they could arrange to invite him up for an interview. Needless to say, after the phone call the invitation never came.

Mr. X is not the only *bête noire* in American academia today. I know of two other doctoral candidates equally bright, equally energetic, equally gifted as teachers, and nearly as well published who have run into the same ebony wall. Their problem is that they specialize in Caribbean literature, another of the little-known but astonishingly vital Third World literatures written in English. The irony of their situation is that the Caribbean is one of the most racially mixed areas of the world, so its writers come in all colors. There is about as much justification for placing Caribbean literature in the context of a black studies program as there is for cramming all of American literature into a one-semester "New England studies" course; it could be done if one were selective enough, but the cuts would remove some of the juiciest meat. Nevertheless, these two students, both of whom are well qualified to teach more orthodox courses as well as their exotic specialty, have been consistently pigeonholed by recruitment committees as unemployable because they are whites working in what is ignorantly believed to be an indelibly black field. The academic mind may need categories for sorting out people according to their interests, but it would be very sad indeed if this natural bureaucratic impulse inevitably led to irrelevant racial criteria being used to assess a candidate's qualifications for teaching an "ethnic" literature. After all, how many Conrad scholars would be out of work if universities insisted they must have Polish ancestry to "qualify" for a job?

I have been told that the job market is even tougher for whites who want to teach African-American literature. The big urban universities won't touch them, state colleges fear rocking the racial boat by making a "controversial" appointment, and the small independent schools would rather not offer such courses than hire a white to teach them. Even though there are plenty of jobs available (about 10% of the vacancies reported in the MLA *Job Information List* are in black literature), it would take unusual courage for an English department to consider recruiting someone without first checking on the color of his skin. This is a disturbing comment on the pervasiveness of this new form of institutionalized racism in American higher education today. Since there are not enough black Ph.D.'s to satisfy the growing demand, one practical consequence is that students at many colleges and universities are not being given the opportunity to study African-American literature. For the sake of English studies in general and Black studies in particular, one can only hope that the day will eventually arrive when the words "equal opportunity employer" no longer mean "whites in black literature need not apply." But until that miracle happens, English and comparative literature departments would do well to scrutinize carefully the applications of young scholars of any color who are working in non-American Black letters, for these unusual men and women can add an exciting, new international dimension to any literature program.

Desert Gold: Irrigation Schemes for Ending the Book Drought

The 1980s appear to have been a decade of glory for African literature. There were clear signs that works by African authors were finally becoming more widely known outside Africa and that this was happening not just in university classrooms but among intelligent lay readers too. The biggest names—Soyinka, Achebe, Ngugi, Senghor, Sembène—were so frequently in the news that they began to enter the standard vocabulary of Western media discourse on modern literature, and highbrow literary magazines and journals were eager to carry interviews with them as well as appraisals of their latest books. With this heightened level of international visibility came instant respectability or at least increased notoriety, and such fame inevitably brought rich rewards: prestigious professorships, honorary degrees, even the Nobel Prize for Literature. Indeed, the Eighties could be said to have been African literature's golden age of recognition and acceptance.

But within Africa itself there was not much evidence of this newfound prosperity and enhanced reputation. The gold simply didn't trickle down to the younger writers who stayed at home and carried on their work without much fanfare or encouragement from outside agencies. Publishers overseas displayed little interest in unknown African writers, and some of the big multinational publishing houses that had launched the careers of the first generation of African writers were cutting back drastically on their African operations. Heinemann, for instance, publisher of the highly influential African Writers Series which gave anglophone African writing its first big boost, found itself taken over by British Tyre and Rubber and then by other corporate raiders who were more interested in increasing their profits than in promoting the development of a foreign literature; the African Writers Series was not completely jettisoned, but it was so severely reduced in scope and significance that it ceased to serve as an important outlet for new, experimental writing from Africa. Longman, which had developed its own line of African literature in an attempt to compete with Heinemann, had to scale back its activities and release some of its editors when it couldn't collect millions of pounds in revenues from the Nigerian Central Bank. Most other multinational publishers, perhaps taking their cue from Heinemann and Longman, rapidly lost enthusiasm for entering an African market where significant returns on investment seemed so improbable. So while the outside world was busy courting Africa's leading superstars, the very publishers who had brought those brilliant luminaries to international attention were deliberately turning away from a whole constellation of lesser lights who had emerged in their shadow. The great majority of the second generation of African writers did not benefit materially from the ground-breaking achievements of their predecessors; instead of earning worldwide renown and substantial remuneration, they had to content themselves with whatever tangible rewards could be won at home. For many of them writing for a local audience was not even a paying proposition. They seldom saw silver, much less gold.

One of the consequences of the slowing-down of multinational publishing activity in several parts of Africa was the speeding-up of local publishing, and many commentators saw this as a good thing—comparable, they argued—to the displacement of Coca-Cola by local beverages. Certainly, anything that encourages indigenous economic enterprise seems preferable to an alternative that perpetuates a reliance on foreign industry. It appears to be a simple matter of choosing self-interest over what could be construed as "neoimperialism."

But the consequences for a writer who is put under this kind of market constraint can be quite devastating. In a number of anglophone African countries—most notably Sierra Leone, Ghana, Zambia, Malawi, Botswana, Lesotho, and Swaziland (not to mention Uganda, Ethiopia, and Liberia, whose economies have collapsed after years of military misrule)—there has been no dynamic growth of indigenous publishing to fill the void left by the reduced activity of the multinational firms. In such cases, where neither local pop nor Coca-Cola is available, the writer goes thirsty. And in countries like Kenya, Tanzania, and Zimbabwe, where there has been a significant amount of local publishing (most of it, in Tanzania, in Kiswahili), the national market for books is so small that an author is not likely to gain much from his writings. In these countries a writer may find something to drink, but it won't be enough to sustain him. He'll have to take another job to earn his daily bread. So in most of anglophone Africa the writer who is dependent upon local publishers to issue his books runs the risk of drying up like a raisin in the sun, and in several of these countries he has no realistic hope of becoming a writer at all because indigenous outlets for his work simply do not exist. How many locally published writers of any significance emerged in anglophone Africa in the 1980s in such arid circumstances? If a few did manage to defy the drought, are any of these slender survivors likely to win a Nobel Prize for Literature?

Nigeria and South Africa appear to afford the only examples of vigorous indigenous publishing enterprise in anglophone Africa, but even in these two vastly dissimilar nations there have been problems that have mitigated the degree of success achieved. In Nigeria the proliferation of small, energetic publishing houses has been nothing short of astounding, and since the potential audience for published works in such a heavily populated nation is quite large, a book that catches on, especially at the school level, stands a chance of reaping a handsome profit. But is this profit shared equitably, and in a businesslike fashion, between publisher and author? Unfortunately, the great majority of fledgling Nigerian publishing firms are still no more than cottage industries, and rigorous accounting procedures are seldom adhered to in such "mom and pop" operations. As a consequence, royalties may or may not be paid, depending on the whim of the publisher. In some cases authors will be asked to subsidize publication of their own work, and this outlay will not be retrievable later on, even if the book turns out to be a bestseller. In recent years there has also been a good deal of book piracy in Nigeria, particularly of school textbooks, so authors who do create a marketable product may get cheated of some of their earnings by unscrupulous buccaneers and blackmarketeers. In response to some of these problems, several Nigerian writers—among them Flora Nwapa and Ken Saro-Wiwa—have established their own publishing houses for producing primarily their own literary works. However, few young writers have the means, aptitude, or inclination to get involved in the physical production, sale, and distribution of what they write; if they do have this impulse, they'll probably wind up as businessmen—publishers, that is—rather than as creative writers. The business climate may be improving in Nigeria, but until local publishing evolves to the point where authors are adequately remunerated for their exertions, those few lucky writers who have a choice will continue to prefer being published abroad. Local publishing, no matter how vigorous, will still play second fiddle to multinational publishing if authors feel they are being swindled by their own countrymen. In such circumstances "neoimperialism" may seem a far more benign economic system than rapacious indigenous capitalism.

In South Africa some of the established local publishing houses have been in existence for a long time and therefore must have maintained satisfactory relationships with their authors. But until recently these older houses have not been very adventurous in seeking out and publishing manuscripts by black, Asian, and so-called "Coloured" writers. Such writers had to wait for the arrival of more courageous publishers such as Ravan Press, Purple Renoster Books, Skotaville Publishers, and the African Writers Assocation, which were willing to take greater risks. Due to repressive legislation governing publishing, for many years there was a very real threat of state censorship, so even these bolder presses had to tread warily. Today, however, the greatest problem for an African writer published in South Africa is that he will stand little chance of being read in most of the rest of Africa. Until apartheid finally is dismantled, most African nations will continue to boycott South African goods, including books. So the South African writer who publishes his work at home will have his primary audience at home and a small secondary audience in the West, but he will effectively cut himself off from readers in most of the rest of Africa, or at least in that portion of the continent north of the Zambezi River, for a few border states such as Zimbabwe, Botswana, and Swaziland still maintain trade links with South Africa.

Of course, except in its political etiology, the isolation of the South African writer is no different from that faced by authors elsewhere in Africa, for nearly all those who publish their work exclusively in their own country will not be read in other parts of the continent, not even in a neighboring country. The distribution of books across national boundaries is a logistical problem that no African publisher has yet conquered. Trade barriers, tariffs, frail transportation networks, and differences in currency and customs may all play a part in hindering the movement of books within Africa, but it is a pity that this kind of intramural communication continues to be obstructed or frustrated. It is bad not just for writers and publishers but also for readers. Indeed, it is bad for Africa as a whole, for it impedes the kind of intellectual exchange necessary for better relations among nations. Africa needs greater unity, not greater fragmentation and balkanization. Voices need to be heard from every corner of the continent, and what better way is there to guarantee the free circulation of ideas than through a flourishing book trade?

So far, we have been looking at the problem of the book drought in Africa from the point of view of the author. Let us now turn our attention to the impact of this drought on the teacher, the student, and the scholar of African literature. What difficulties do the academic consumers of African literature confront today when seeking the best reading matter?

One of the major problems for those involved in teaching or studying African literature in Africa is that of gaining access to primary and secondary sources. Books assigned for courses may not be available in local bookstores or libraries. Books ordered from overseas may be slow in arriving or may be so expensive that students—and teachers!—cannot afford to buy them. Many African universities, recognizing the gravity of this situation, have provided their students with a modest book allowance that enables them to buy needed textbooks, but sometimes inflation eats into this allowance to such an extent that it becomes too modest to be of much assistance; for instance, at the University of Zambia in 1986 the book allowance for literature students had dwindled to such a level that it enabled students to purchase only one title from the African Writers Series. Even so, this was a more generous allowance than was available to students at the University of Sierra Leone who received almost no financial help at all.

For teachers the shortage of books in the classroom poses special problems. In extreme cases, as in several courses at the University of Calabar in Nigeria, for example, teachers had to resort to providing elaborate plot summaries of novels and plays that their students could not obtain. In other words, written literature was being taught without texts. On other campuses, such as the University of Malawi and the University of Ghana, teachers substituted older novels that were available in multiple copies in the university library for newer novels that could not be found at the university bookstore, so instead of teaching, say, Achebe's *Anthills of the Savannah* in a course on African fiction, these instructors might be forced to teach a book like Abrahams's *Mine Boy*.

In a survey of African literature teaching conducted a few years ago at thirty anglophone African universities (see pp. 45-59), I discovered that the books most frequently taught were the following (presented here in rank order, with ties grouped together):

1. Achebe, *Arrow of God*
2. Ngugi, *A Grain of Wheat*
3. Ngugi, *Petals of Blood*
4. Achebe, *A Man of the People*
5. Okot, *Song of Lawino*
6. Ngugi/Githae-Mugo, *The Trial of Dedan Kimathi*
7. Armah, *The Beautyful Ones Are Not Yet Born*
    Soyinka, *The Interpreters*
9. Soyinka, *Kongi's Harvest*
10. Okigbo, *Labyrinths*
11. Sembène, *God's Bits of Wood*
12. Achebe, *Things Fall Apart*
13. Soyinka, *Idanre and Other Poems*
14. Ngugi/Ngugi, *I Will Marry When I Want*
    La Guma, *A Walk in the Night*
    Fugard, *Statements...*
17. Sutherland, *The Marriage of Anansewa*
18. Bâ, *So Long a Letter*
    Beti, *The Poor Christ of Bomba*
20. Armah, *Fragments*
21. Sembène, *Xala*
    Armah, *Two Thousand Seasons*
    La Guma, *In the Fog of the Seasons' End*
24. Ngugi, *Devil on the Cross*
    Okara, *The Fisherman's Invocation*
    Brutus, *Letters to Martha*
    Oyono, *The Old Man and the Medal*
28. Beti, *Mission to Kala*
    Ngugi, *The River Between*
    Soyinka, *The Lion and the Jewel*
    Oyono, *Houseboy*
32. Rotimi, *The Gods Are Not to Blame*
    Achebe, *Morning Yet on Creation Day*

Brutus, *A Simple Lust*
Clark, *Song of a Goat*
36. Soyinka, *A Shuttle in the Crypt*
La Guma, *Time of the Butcherbird*
Soyinka, *Collected Plays*
Okara, *The Voice*
Soyinka, *Madmen and Specialists*
Aidoo, *Anowa*

If we study this list with care, certain conclusions become inescapable. First, all the titles on the list have been published by multinational publishers. True, in some countries there may be local editions of the novels of Achebe, the novels and plays of Ngugi, the poetry of Okot and Okigbo, and the plays of Sutherland and Aidoo, but the only editions of these works that are available throughout Africa are those issued by a multinational firm.

Second, the publisher most frequently represented on the list is Heinemann, which can claim nine of the top ten texts, sixteen of the top twenty, and thirty of the full list of forty-one titles. The African Writers Series obviously is a major force not only in African literature publishing but also in African literature teaching. It is no exaggeration to say that it would be virtually impossible to teach a survey course on modern African literature today without having a good number of their books represented on the syllabus. Other publishers such as Oxford University Press, Longman, and Methuen are represented on the list by a few titles each, but they do not come close to challenging Heinemann's paramountcy.

Third, virtually all these books were published some time ago, half of them in the 1960s. The newest title is Mariama Bâ's *So Long a Letter*, which first appeared in English translation in 1981. Such a time-lag may be a normal feature of canon formation in any literature, for it reflects a kind of institutional inertia or resistance on the part of instructors to changing a familiar curriculum. The assumption may be that the cream will eventually rise to the top, that those masterpieces written today and tomorrow will ultimately find their niche somewhere in the hierarchy, displacing and demoting less artistic works written in an earlier era. In short, the good literature inevitably will drive out the bad.

But is this a reasonable assumption given the extracurricular biases governing book selection by teachers? Wouldn't we also have to posit a corollary that future masterpieces would have a chance of entering the teaching canon only if they were published in paperback by a multinational firm, preferably Heinemann? What chance would a text have of gaining pan-African canonical status if it were published solely in Harare, Nairobi, Lagos, or Accra? How could such a book be ordered by a campus bookshop in another country? How would teachers elsewhere in Africa even know of its existence?

These questions have important implications for the future of African literature studies, for if Heinemann is still king (or king-maker) in most of anglophone Africa, and if the Heinemann African Writers Series is now a shrunken organ of production issuing fewer and fewer titles each year, how will the new masterpieces make their way into print? Will the beautiful ones still be born? Or will they be stillborn, strangled by the economic umbilical cord that ties them to a remote, alien, corporate empire, the foreign managers of which do not particularly care whether they live or die? Are African literature teachers destined to continue prescribing the same old classics year after year because fewer new options are now flowing through the labyrinths of the international publishing pipeline? Will a prolonged African book drought produce a premature petrification of the African literature canon?

The pessimism underlying such questions is exacerbated when one examines the plight of the African literature researcher in Africa today. Few African university libraries have been able to keep up with the explosion of commentary on modern African literature. Starved for funds and denied access to tightly controlled sources of foreign exchange, these libraries have not been able to order the latest critical and scholarly books published in Europe or America, much less in other parts of Africa. Worse yet, they have not been able to order academic journals from abroad, so the faculty and students who find themselves entirely dependent upon such institutional libraries have absolutely no access to the latest international scholarship published in their field. It should be understood that I am not referring here only to writings produced by non-African scholars. Many of Africa's most distinguished academics regularly publish articles and reviews in international scholarly journals that are never seen on their own campuses. So Africa is being denied some of the best of African thought on African literature because underfunded African university libraries do not have the means to purchase key journals from abroad.

Sadder still, the inadequacy of these libraries is making it increasingly difficult for African scholars to contribute effectively to ongoing critical and theoretical debates in African literature because it is impossible for them to keep up with the latest arguments. This is one reason why so many African scholars look for opportunities to spend a sabbatical year abroad at an institution where they will have access to recent publications in their field. Such a quest should not be misconstrued as a form of academic opportunism or rampant careerism. For some it is sheerly a matter of professional survival: one must go overseas to find the equipment necessary to function successfully in a competitive environment at home. For others it is a chance simply to drink deep at the Pierian spring, a treat that any thirsty academic recognizes as wholly justifiable. The majority of these visiting scholars do not seek permanent positions abroad. They just want temporary refreshment and renewal—a genesis, not an exodus. They have no desire to contribute to the brain drain from Africa; rather, they want their brains refilled so that they can better help their own people. Basically, they are seeking access to vital information that they lack at home. It is the drought, not the unholy dollar, that has turned them into pilgrims.

But it would take a massive airlift to carry all these would-be alhajis to academic meccas overseas, and such moneys might be better spent transporting the tools to the scholars rather than the scholars to the tools. How many books could be purchased for the price of an airticket from Lagos to Los Angeles, Accra to Austin, Maseru to Madison, Nairobi to New York? How many journal subscriptions could be maintained on a single sabbatical salary, no matter how small? Maybe it would be better for African universities to invest a greater portion of their meager resources in the acquisition of academic hardware than in the dispersal of human software. Would foreign pilgrimages be necessary if African scholars could slake their thirst at indigenous oases fed by a network of pipelines to the rest of the world's Pierian springs? Establishing and servicing such connections might be difficult and expensive, but with such an irrigation system in place, all it would take to survive the most terrible drought would be efficient, well-engineered plumbing.

However, this may be too utopian a solution to a very mundane problem that has its origin in the grinding poverty that besets all too many of Africa's nation-states. It is doubtful that Africa could afford the technology needed to tap into the world's store of knowledge. This may be a long-range goal worth pursuing, but in the meantime some short-term measures are required to address immediate problems. Here is where foreign aid could prove salutory. So, to turn the question around, let us ask not how Africa can help itself but how we in the outside world can help Africa. Specifically, how can those of us in the West who are involved in African literature studies assist in alleviating the current book drought in Africa?

The answer appears simple: send books and journals to African libraries. But the mechanisms for effecting this sort of philanthropy require pondering, for there is some sensitivity in Africa to being the recipient of the West's unwanted or secondhand surplus goods, and sometimes well-intentioned gifts of educational materials have been criticized by their recipients as examples of "book-dumping"—equivalent, that is, to garbage disposal or to the removal to Africa of European and American toxic wastes. Gifts are welcome if they meet urgent needs, but they are of questionable value if they are regarded as unnecessary or harmful by those to whom they are directed.

One way of assuring that gifts are welcome is to find out what is most desperately in demand and then to work to supply that. This can be done easily enough through correspondence with colleagues at African universities. Several years ago Professor Eustace Palmer, Chairman of the English Department at Fourah Bay College in Sierra Leone, appealed to faculty and students at The University of Texas at Austin to supply specific texts that were assigned readings in English, American, and African literature courses in his Department but were not available in any local bookstores in Sierra Leone. The response was heartening. Students, especially at end of term, were more than willing to donate novels, plays, and volumes of poetry that they had just finished using in their own courses, and several hundred books were soon on their way to Freetown. This kind of targeted aid is most effective in addressing educational needs and is greatly appreciated; it also gives a good deal of satisfaction to the donors, who feel they are materially assisting fellow students in Africa.

Another type of aid can be rendered by professional academic associations in the West. Most teachers of African literature are members of literary organizations or area studies associations or both. Such dues-paying members ought to insist that the books and journals published by these organizations be given free of charge to African university libraries, even if the cost of such donations would drive up dues. There are fewer than 125 universities in all of Africa, so the price of such philanthropy is not unduly high. Associations concerned specifically with African studies have a moral obligation to join the campaign to alleviate the book drought in the area of the world that is the focus of their studies.

Scholars can also make donations of a more personal sort. Anyone who writes or edits a book on African literature ought to see to it that a copy of that book is given to every African university or at the very least to every university library in parts of Africa that are discussed in the book. In a sense, this is more than an expected courtesy; it is a method of repaying an intellectual debt owed to Africa by the Africanist scholar.

There are numerous ways of financing such arrangements, but perhaps the simplest is for an author to forfeit royalties until the costs incurred by his publisher in supplying copies to African university libraries are fully discharged. This may seem an expensive gesture, but I doubt that many scholars are dependent upon royalties for their livelihood. Most books on African literature are not bestsellers anyway, so the amount of income lost really will not matter much in the long run. And besides, consider the alternative: if your book does not get to Africa, if it is not available to scholars and students anywhere on the African continent, what contribution can your scholarship be said to be making to African literature studies? Isn't it pointless to publish a book that does not reach its primary audience? Why write on African literature if you do not wish to engage in a meaningful dialogue with Africans themselves? Why be an Africanist if you have no commitment to Africa's future?

Obviously, the book drought in Africa is too vast a problem to be solved by individual donations of a few books and journals, but in conditions of extreme deprivation and scarcity, every drop in the bucket has the potential for sustaining intellectual life and therefore is worth its weight in gold.

Research Requirements

The Six Commandments

For the past fifteen years I have been editing *Research in African Literatures (RAL)*, a journal that publishes scholarship on the oral and written literatures of Africa. During this time *RAL* has grown from a biannual publication of about 100 pages per issue to a quarterly containing 160 pages per issue. This threefold increase in size reflects to some extent not only the rapid growth of scholarly interest in these literatures but also the concomitant development of African literary studies as a recognized discipline in universities throughout the world, especially within Africa itself. Today quite a few scholars can support themselves by teaching, studying, and writing about African verbal arts; twenty-five years ago this was not the case. *RAL* thus may be seen as an academic spinoff of the African revolution—that is, as a byproduct of the same forces that have transformed the African continent since the process of decolonization began. The journal has survived and thrived because more scholars have been free to devote their time and intellectual energy to exploring African expressive traditions that previously were inadequately examined, blithely ignored, or deliberately avoided. By providing a forum for articulating ideas about new or unapprehended verbal manifestations of Africa's rich cultural heritage, *RAL* has helped to bring into being a substantial literature on African literatures.

This metaliterature has itself changed over the course of time. One happy consequence of rapid disciplinary growth is that the quality of scholarly commentary on African literatures has been gradually improving. *RAL* receives many more publishable articles today than it did when it began, and even though we have much more space at our disposal now, we simply cannot publish everything that may be fit for print. So the proliferation of scholarly activity forces us to be far more selective than in the past; difficult decisions must be made every month, separating not just the sheep from the goats, but frequently the wooliest sheep from those with slightly thinner fleeces, so that only the best enter our pages. Of course, some would say that this is as it should be: after all, a fundamental law of the academic jungle is that only the fittest should survive. But I sometimes wonder, when sending off a letter of rejection to a perfectly competent scholar who unfortunately has not yet evolved into a super-sheep, if discouraging the fit is the best method for bettering a breed. High selectivity may be a terribly wasteful way to develop a discipline, for it may lead to a wholesale slaughter of innocents, the promising and pedestrian alike. Perhaps the wildest as well as the wooliest need to be nurtured, if only to preserve a streak of originality in future generations. Not all the best generative propensities will pass through a very tight screen.

But the fact remains that we have a fixed number of pages per issue so we cannot accommodate every worthwhile article that reaches us. Indeed, we are forced to return as much as ninety percent of the material submitted, and each year the proportion of submissions we print seems to grow smaller. If this trend continues, we may well end up a victim of our own overspecialized tendencies, rather like the Irish elk, whose impressive antlers grew to such a prodigious size that it could no longer compete with smaller, more maneuverable forest creatures and therefore became extinct. Present success, in other words, could spell future doom, particularly if we do not develop a capacity for flexibility, enabling us to make our way adroitly through whatever wilderness of words we may encounter. We must adapt to new circumstances or die.

So, it is with an editor's eye on adaptation, natural selection, evolution, and survival that I would like to offer some suggestions to scholars of African literatures who may wish to achieve a small measure of academic immortality by publishing their work in *Research in African Literatures* before this living organ becomes part of the fossil record. I can speak for no other journal and no other editors, not even for those hard-working masochists who continue to read and evaluate manuscripts for *RAL*; they may, and usually do, have strong opinions of their own, and I cannot pretend to represent the full diversity of those views here. It should also be understood that I am basing my comments on a vast ocean of scholarly literature that many of you will never have occasion to wade through, mainly because much of this effluent will never make its way into solid print. I find myself in a position to offer a few modest prescriptions for success only because I have seen so many flagrant examples of failure. Since I do not have time to present a complete taxonomy of authorial transgressions, I shall focus only on the most important matters, delivering my remarks, in the oracular style of Moses, as a list of holy commandments. First, a few words to the folklorists:

1. BE IMAGINATIVE! I place this commandment foremost because it is the one most frequently violated. Too much scholarship on African oral literatures in conceptually timid, offering routine proofs of tired formulations devised in the past to account for phenomena observed elsewhere in the world. The average scholar appears to feel a compulsion to demonstrate a loyalty, not to the primary data he is attempting to codify and explicate, but rather to the secondary literature that has grown up around such data in the last century. When the old wooden shoe, usually manufactured in Europe or the United States, does not quite fit the shape of the idiosyncratic African foot, unimaginative scholars try to force it on anyway, confining their attention to locating precisely where it pinches rather than going on to devise more appropriate footwear from the ground up. As a consequence, African folklore becomes little more than a foreign laboratory for testing the limitations of Western theories of folklore. The theories do not derive from the inherent nature of the observable data but are applied to the

data externally in the hope or expectation that they will do justice—or at least do no injustice—to the African verbal realities being scrutinized. Secondhand theories are the refuge of the unimaginative, second-rate scholar who doesn't have the courage to branch off and go out on a limb of his own.

2. BE RESPONSIBLE! It is not enough, of course, to be creative or ingenious in dealing with fresh data. One must demonstrate an awareness of the issues that the new data raise and be able to place one's own contribution to discussion of those issues in a context that will make them comprehensible to others concerned with similar matters. In other words, one should seek to advance international folklore scholarship, not just African folklore scholarship, in one's formulations, but to do this well, one must know intimately the traditions of scholarship in which others work. The uninformed scholar, no matter how creative he may be, will find himself handicapped by his inability to speak competently in a recognized international academic idiom. Moreover, he will not succeed in communicating his own ideas effectively if he fails to take account of what others have already said on the same or related subjects. He needs to do his homework before he does his field work, so that he will be capable of recognizing his own genuine discoveries and will not dissipate his intellectual energy in redundant efforts to reinvent the wheel. No scholar can be truly imaginative unless he is thoroughly responsible.

3. BE COOPERATIVE, if possible. In the rapidly expanding world of folklore scholarship, it can be difficult to keep up with all the latest ideas. New publications from one part of the world may be unavailable in another part or may be written in a language that renders them inaccessible. Information about important related developments in other disciplines may not reach the folklorist immediately. Serious

social, political, and economic problems at home or abroad may further impede the free flow of ideas. In some countries fieldwork may be restricted or even forbidden.

One consequence of such impediments to responsible research has been a serious imbalance in the scholarship produced on African oral literatures. Western scholarship has tended to be top-heavy with theory but thin in data, whereas African scholarship has tended to be bottom-heavy with data but thin in theory. Given the shape of the world today, these tendencies may continue to subvert folklore scholarship unless steps are taken soon to restore some balance. Western scholars, for instance, might benefit from fuller instruction in African languages and enhanced opportunities for prolonged fieldwork, while African scholars might expand their theoretical knowledge by spending some time in residence at a major European or American folklore center.

A simpler and less expensive solution would be to facilitate communication between Western and African scholars so that significant collaborative research projects could be undertaken that would build upon the strengths of all the parties concerned. Teamwork of this sort could be mutually enriching and could result in better-informed scholarship. It would not be a matter merely of two or more heads being better than one; rather, close collaboration would prove that one coherent and carefully articulated body of opinion on a subject is far better than any number of half-baked notions offered at random from various quarters. Cooperation might well turn out to be the most expeditious route to imaginative, responsible research in African oral literatures. At least it is worth a try.

These, then, are my three editorial exhortations to the folklorists:

> Be Imaginative.
> Be Responsible.
> Be Cooperative.

In short, IRC. I hope that all future contributors of folklore studies to *RAL* will take these IRC-some recommendations to heart and that better research in African oral literatures will be the result.

To scholars working primarily on African written literatures, I have a different set of suggestions, which I shall also present in hierarchical order, starting at the top.

1. BE FACTUAL! Critics of written literatures do not need to be encouraged to use their imagination. Much too frequently this is all they have at their disposal, for they haven't bothered to examine the most elementary contextual markers that root a literary work in a particular time and place. Dates, geographical circumstances, and biographical details bore them, for they would rather dabble in what they imagine to be "higher" matters, such as interpretation and evaluation of texts. Yet without a sound knowledge of basic facts, they are not likely to get very far off the ground, and some of their loftiest theories may prove vaporous under the glare of illuminating contradictory evidence in the form of indisputable concrete realities. The scholar who steadfastly refuses to look behind or beyond the text runs the risk of playing meaningless verbal games in a social void, games which obscure the very truths he purports to seek. He should come down to earth before he starts reaching for the stars.

2. BE ARGUMENTATIVE! Commentators on African written literatures should aim to prove a point and therefore should adopt a rhetorical strategy appropriate to the line of argument being pursued. Serious debaters addressing complex issues will need to reinforce their chosen position with mounds of solid evidence. Unlike some poets, they cannot merely "state the bare fact and let it sing" (Brutus 136), for there may be many facts and many different ways of singing them. The objective should be to find the best notes, select the right register, and then amplify the pitch to such an extent that other, weaker voices are drowned out. Of course, one cannot

win an argument simply by shouting; this is not what is being advocated here. Rather, the scholar is being advised to prepare his case with care, ensuring that the greatest volume of irrefutable evidence is on his side. To do his work effectively, he must be well-briefed and able to weigh the opinions of others, particularly those with whom he elects to disagree, so that he can undercut their arguments and also counter objections to his own views. In sum the scholar must be a highly skilled rhetorician with a distinct point of view.

3. BE TRUE! There is a temptation in any debate to overstate a case in order to win more points. This can be done by tailoring the evidence to fit the argument, stretching it a bit here, trimming it a bit there, until a near-perfect match between subject and syllogism is achieved. In this kind of creative enterprise, logic can be bent out of shape to serve predetermined ends, so that the final result is less a demonstration of proof than a confirmation of prior prejudice. The researcher is hunting for a specific configuration and miraculously finds it wherever he looks; the raw data is processed until it leads inexorably to the cooked conclusion. Such argumentation, conscious or unconscious, is bad scholarship, for it eschews objectivity. The scholar wants most of all to win the debate, not to discover verifiable truth, so he equivocates, compromising his data and in the process perverting his own profession. True scholars must resist such temptations and remain true to the highest principles of their discipline.

So my three editorial injunctions to scholars of African written literatures are the following:

Be Factual.

Be Argumentative.

Be True.

In short, be FAT! Scholars who do not aspire to be heavyweights in the field of African literatures may of course disregard these commandments and go their own wasteful way, but I hope they will never try to foist their ill-nourished ideas on readers of *RAL*—at least not while the present editor is still alive and well and watching what they eat as well as what they ask others to swallow.

Towards a Nigerian Literary Archive

When I attended the Ibadan Conference on the African Novel in July of 1978, I found myself sitting on a hot seat. Word had spread that I was trying to acquire the newly discovered manuscript of Amos Tutuola's *The Palm-Wine Drinkard* for the Humanities Research Center at The University of Texas at Austin, and many Nigerian literary scholars, some of whom had never before displayed any interest in Tutuola's works, expressed shock and outrage that such a brazen act of cultural brigandage could be contemplated in the postcolonial era. Several of them likened my efforts to the nineteenth century looting of Benin or, worse yet, to the trafficking in human cargo that occurred during the days of the slave trade. I was seen as the modern equivalent of Long John Silver, Jesse James, and Simon Legree rolled into one. I must admit that it was not the most comfortable conference I have ever attended but it surely was the most memorable.

To the charge that I was trying to arrange for a Texas literary archive to acquire valuable manuscript materials, I had to plead guilty. I felt it was essential that the *Drinkard* manuscript, as well as Tutuola's other papers, be preserved in conditions that would ensure their longevity and guarantee their accessibility to future generations of literary scholars. The Humanities Research Center at The University of Texas, with current holdings of roughly 800,000 rare books and six million manuscripts, ranks as the leading repository in the United States (and possibly the entire Western world) for twentieth-century literary materials; so it seemed—to me, at least, then—to be the right institution to approach about acquiring Tutuola's manuscripts. Not only would they take good care of them, but they would also be able to pay Tutuola well for them, I figured. Thus, it would be in the best interests of both Tutuola and future African literary scholarship for these manuscripts to wind up in Austin, Texas.

I was operating on the assumption that no Nigerian university library or archive would be sufficiently interested in such materials to compensate Tutuola for them at their "market" value, which I imagined to be quite high. After all, Tutuola had been a prophet without honor in his own country for more than a quarter of a century, and I had seen no evidence to suggest that his critical reputation at home had risen appreciably in recent years. Indeed, considering his importance not just as an anomaly (some would say "freak") in the history of African literature in English, but more significantly as a pioneer in the Nigerian literary movement, it was surprising to me that so few of his countrymen, especially fellow Yorubas, had taken a serious interest in him as a literary artist of a very rare and special kind. As far as I knew, no Nigerian doctoral dissertations or master's theses on him had ever been written and only one Nigerian scholar was considering writing a book on him. I had even heard that in the literature departments of some Nigerian universities his works were not even being read.

This astonishingly supine neglect at home contrasted sharply with the amount of interest and scholarly activity his writings had continued to generate abroad. Four books had already been published on him by French, German, and American scholars, and there had been numerous articles, theses, and conference papers in which various aspects of his work had been discussed. Tutuola, it appeared, was more an international literary figure than a Nigerian one. A naive outsider aware of this puzzling discrepancy between Tutuola's world reputation and his national reputation might be forgiven for wondering whether such an institution as the Nigerian National Archives would even have been willing to purchase any of his manuscripts.

The Nigerian scholars at the conference proved most of my assumptions to be wrong. They asserted that though it might be "fashionable" for outsiders to assume Tutuola was still neglected and maligned at home, Nigerians were well aware of the contribution he had made to the development of their national literary culture. In fact, Chinua Achebe had recently inaugurated a series of distinguished lectures at the University of Ibadan by speaking on Tutuola. Moreover, Nigerians did not want to see valuable Nigerian cultural artifacts of any kind—manuscripts, paintings, statues, masks—carried off and given a permanent home abroad. They felt that their own institutions should, could, and would shoulder the responsibility of preserving such treasures. Foreign aid or interference in the task of conserving major monuments of Nigerian culture would no longer be tolerated.

Several academics at the University of Ife had already taken steps to ensure that *The Palm-Wine Drinkard* manuscript would be deposited at the University of Ife Library. Enlisting the support of the Vice-Chancellor of the University, they had arranged that a substantial sum be offered to Tutuola for the manuscript and that Tutuola himself be given an academic appointment at the University for a term. This kind of recognition of Tutuola's worth and stature as a writer was concrete proof that he was no longer an artist without honor in his own country.

This last point made their case very convincing, and after the conference I cabled the Humanities Research Center at The University of Texas instructing them to stop negotiating to acquire both the *Drinkard* manuscript and an earlier manuscript of Tutuola's which I had located in the files of a British publisher of photography books. This would enable the University of Ife Library to purchase the second manuscript too, which in some ways was more interesting than the *Drinkard* manuscript because it was older and had never been published. If the University of Ife Library were to acquire the rest of Tutuola's papers, particularly the files of correspondence he has very carefully preserved for the past thirty years, it could automatically become the world center of Tutuola studies.

But perhaps Nigerians should be asking if this is really enough. Should the effort to preserve important Nigerian literary materials stop with one library's acquisition of Amos Tutuola's papers? Shouldn't other valuable manuscripts, typescripts, galleys, page proofs, and books be pursued with equal determination and enthusiasm? If they are not, Nigeria will have won one small nationalistic battle but it will lose the wider war for cultural conservation. Indeed, if further action is not taken swiftly, future generations of Nigerian literary scholars may find it necessary to travel to London, New York, or some other foreign metropolis to consult primary documents in their own national literary history.

What I am suggesting is that Nigeria needs its own Humanities Research Center, its own archive devoted to the preservation of significant literary materials. One might argue that the National Archives can adequately serve such a purpose, but I doubt that they would pursue such papers as zealously as they do newspapers, government documents, and civil service files. The National Archives, like government archives elsewhere, seem to be interested primarily in preserving materials relevant to the political history of the nation. While they might accept donations of literary papers, they probably would not actively solicit such contributions or devote more than a minimal amount of their energy and resources to endeavors peripheral to what they define as the main purpose of their existence.

Some will say that university libraries should take the initiative in pursuing such papers, as Ife did with Tutuola's manuscripts. This would seem to make good sense inasmuch as many of the leading writers in the country hold university appointments and could easily be contacted by university librarians who might encourage them to deposit their papers in a campus archive. But while I was in Nigeria, I was told that a few university librarians who had already tried to build up literary collections through friendly persuasion of this sort had not met with success. One problem was purely financial. They had to rely on voluntary contributions because they could not offer remuneration to authors out of library funds that had been earmarked for the acquisition of books. University libraries will always be faced with this kind of dilemma—should they spend all their money on materials that will benefit the university community at large, or should they commit a certain portion of their budget to acquisitions that will be of use only to a very small number of specialized scholars? One can predict that in the constrained financial circumstances in which most university libraries find themselves today, democracy will always win out over elitism. The books will always be acquired before the manuscripts.

So it would seem that a separate institution, or perhaps a sub-unit of an existing institution, should be set up, given its own annual budget, and charged with the responsibility of preserving Nigeria's literary heritage. It wouldn't have to be a lavishly funded or elegantly housed archive. A few rooms in a library or museum would probably suffice at the outset. But it should employ a director whose fulltime job is to solicit, collect, and preserve manuscripts, books, tape recordings, photographs, films, and other materials related to the development of literary culture in Nigeria. In a sense, it would be the equivalent of a museum of Nigerian art, the only difference being in the nature of the materials collected. In an age when most African governments do not have to be persuaded of the value of preserving outstanding works of art made of metal, wood, or canvas, certainly some would see the merit of conserving equally important masterworks done on paper or celluloid. Who could argue that a statue of Queen Elizabeth sculpted by Ben Enwonwu is more worthy of preservation than, say, the original manuscript of Okigbo's *Heavensgate*. Both are important cultural artifacts. Both need to be safeguarded so that future generations will not be deprived of the pleasure of examining them.

There are some writers, of course, who place no value on their manuscripts and working papers. To them, it is only the finished product—the bound book or published poem—that really matters. The rest is merely waste paper fit for the dustbin. Such writers fail to understand or appreciate the crucial importance of primary documents in future literary scholarship.

Fifty years from now, when scholars are attempting to edit the complete works of Wole Soyinka, they will find it extremely difficult to establish accurate texts for *The Interpreters* and *Season of Anomy* (to mention only two works flawed by numerous misprints) if none of the author's manuscripts and none of the publisher's proofs are available for study. Others who may be interested in larger matters such as the process of creation, the tactics of translation, or the impact of technological change (e.g., literacy) on traditions of verbal art will be sorely disappointed if the papers of such writers as Okigbo, Okara, and Fagunwa have not been saved. And anyone attempting to write a literary biography of an author will be severly handicapped if no one has bothered to collect that author's letters. Writers who value their reputation and who do not wish to be misquoted, misinterpreted, and misunderstood in the years to come should not be careless about their papers today. Indeed, they should eagerly support the establishment of an archive where they can deposit such documents.

Naturally, some writers may abhor the idea of letting researchers poke about in their personal papers. It may seem a violation of basic human rights, a gross invasion of their privacy. Yet such writers should realize that the price one has to pay for literary fame, or any other kind of human distinction for that matter, is submission to prolonged public nosiness about one's private life. People are curious to know more about celebrities and will begin to invent details if no hard data exist. Very few verifiable facts have been discovered about Shakespeare's life, yet libraries are full of biographies of him, some of which attribute all his writings to other authors! The writer who cares about what will be said of him in the future should not try to conceal or suppress significant biographical information. If he is famous enough, if he is destined to join the literary immortals, as perhaps a handful of living Nigerian authors are, then nothing will prevent later literary scholars from exhuming most of the important facts anyway. The writer should collaborate in his own apotheosis by leaving his academic gravediggers a bunch of keys, if only to forestall the possibility of all these sealed subterranean facts being garbled when brought to light. Some scholars need help, a shuttle *into* the crypt.

Also, it should be pointed out that the author who deposits his papers in an archive has the right to place restrictions on their use. Mark Twain insisted that certain of his manuscripts should not be published until so many years after his death. Edith Wharton did not want her contemporaries to read some of her personal correspondence so she specified that a particular box of her letters should not be opened until a full century had passed. Writers who are worried about inadvertently betraying the confidence of friends can take legal steps to ensure that such people will not be embarrassed by hasty posthumous revelations. An author is best able to protect his own rights as well as the rights of his associates and heirs if he personally attends to the disposal of his papers. A Nigerian literary archive could facilitate the formalization of such arrangements.

There is an urgent need to establish a Nigerian literary archive now because a number of important documents have already been lost to libraries overseas. To cite just a few examples, the Library of the School of Oriental and African Studies (SOAS) at the University of London has acquired the galley proofs of Okigbo's *Labyrinths* (Ms. English 326710), a typescript along with page proofs of Achebe's *Beware, Soul Brother* (Ms. English 329716), and a typescript (probably the publisher's own "fair copy" rather than the original) of Amos Tutuola's *Ajaiyi and His Inherited Poverty* (Ms. English 288001). More startling still, it holds the typescript of an unpublished English translation of the late D.O. Fagunwa's *Àdiitú Olódùmarè* (Ms. English 326709) which had been done by Fagunwa himself with the assistance of someone named E.M. Milne (whose name, incidentally, has been penciled out on the title page). One can also find the papers of several other African writers in this library—most notably the typescripts of Dennis Brutus's *A Simple Lust* and of some of Ngugi wa Thiong'o's short stories and novels, including the complete texts of *Weep Not, Child* and *A Grain of Wheat*. Next door to the SOAS

Library, the British Library (formerly called the British Museum) holds a typescript of Wole Soyinka's poem "Idanre" with a very interesting handwritten note concerning the significance of the Möbius strip scrawled on the back of the last page; as far as I know, this is the only working draft of any of his works that Soyinka himself has ever allowed to be preserved in a literary archive. Are there no Nigerian scholars who wish to study such papers? I am sure there are quite a number who would like to be given the opportunity to do so, and I am equally certain that the amount of money that would have to be spent transporting them all to London and maintaining them there throughout the period of their research would be sufficient to fund a Nigerian literary archive for several years. Establishing a local research facility of this sort would therefore save the Nigerian Government of a lot of Naira!

One may ask how it happens that so many important African literary manuscripts have already been obtained by British libraries? To a few paranoid observers, this may appear to be evidence of some kind of nefarious neocolonial plot, but I suspect it is nothing of the kind. Rather, it seems more likely that one or two professional archivists in Britain, on noticing that no one was making an effort to preserve such documents, offered to put their facilities at the disposal of British publishers who were in the business of publishing original creative works by African authors. That is, the archivists probably encouraged the publishers (or perhaps postage-conscious publishers took it upon themselves) to inquire whether the authors would be willing to allow such materials to be deposited in certain British libraries instead of returned to them after publication. Several authors, placing no value on what they may have considered as the detritus of their art, apparently agreed to this arrangement, and some of them may have been paid for the papers they gave up. One could check up on this by asking the authors themselves, or their heirs, or possibly even the publishers or archivists concerned. Someone must have a record of each transaction, for papers housed in public archives undoubtedly are not stolen goods. I believe a responsible investigation of this matter will reveal that the primary motive behind such British archival accessions was honest conservation, not ruthless exploitation. Professional archivists, who spend their lives accumulating and preserving documents, must feel that they have a sacred duty to ensure that important papers do not get lost. If they were made aware that an archive somewhere in Africa was committed to acquiring African literary manuscripts, they probably would not bother tapping the resources of their own institutions to make such acquisitions. What matters most to them is preservation, not location, of the documents.

Which brings me to my final point. When Nigeria ultimately establishes a national literary archive—as it no doubt will sometime in the future, if the present generation of literary scholars fails to lobby effectively for it today—I hope this archive will be Nigerian only in name, for it should be truly international (or at least pan-African) in scope. There are many African writers today—South Africans, Ugandans, Guineans, Ghanaians, etc.— who are living in exile for one reason or another, and they may not wish or expect their papers ever to be collected in their homeland. There is a real danger that such papers may never be collected at all unless an African archive steps in and does the job. Elsewhere in Africa there are writers, living and dead, whose papers are likely simply to vanish because no one is bothering to gather and preserve them. I imagine that quite a few West Indian and African-American writers would be delighted to be able to deposit their papers in an African archive. Indeed, the field is wide open, and it is high time that this kind of work be done in a systematic fashion somewhere in Africa. If Nigeria wishes to take a leading role in safeguarding the literary heritage of the Black world, it should found an institution dedicated to preserving for future generations the recorded thoughts and utterances of those creatively gifted individuals who have shaped the intellectual and imaginative life of their times.

The Future of African Literary Studies*

First, I wish to thank the conveners of this conference for inviting me here and giving me this opportunity to speak to you. It is not often that we who live in the Texas bush get a chance to visit centers of culture nowadays, especially those in other oil-poor regions of the earth. So I feel somewhat out of place in this setting, partly because it seems more than a little bizarre in these hard times for an outsider like me to come all this distance to address insiders like you about your own literature. Indeed, I was worried for a while that the immigration authorities at Murtala Muhammed Airport might intervene and declare me an illegal import or might search through my bags looking for illicit intellectual goods, suspecting—as many of my colleagues back home do—that I am engaged in an eccentric, infamous, or wholly unnecessary enterprise, equivalent to carrying kola to Calabar. To those who fear some kind of international conspiracy is behind all this, I can only swear that I am not an agent working in behalf of alien forces intent on the recolonization of African literature and that, quite honestly, I am just as surprised as anyone else that I am standing before you today. I have been given a totally unexpected honor, and I want to assure you in advance that I do not intend to abuse your kindness and hospitality by utilizing this platform as a launching pad for conventional critical barbs and arrows. Some of you may have suffered too much of that kind of bombardment from me already, and I did not come here to add to your annoyance or discomfort, at least not by conscious design. If what I say offends anyone, please forgive me. Texans are not known for their good manners; we are crude, clumsy

* Delivered at the Sixth Annual University of Calabar International Conference on African Literature and the English Language, 1986.

people wearing large and heavy boots, so when dancing in a big crowd, we find it virtually impossible to avoid trampling on the sensitivities of others, even on those occasions when we don't mean to do any harm.

I want to speak to you today not about the past or the present but about the future—specifically, the future of African literary studies. Frankly, I'm a little uneasy about what I see in my crystal ball, and I want to share this uneasiness with you, if only to pass the burden from my mind to yours so we can carry it together. Perhaps one question that those of us who study African literatures ought to put to ourselves occasionally is this: what kind of responsibility do we have to future generations of African literature scholars? What will the grandchildren of our grandchildren, those unborn kin we will never see, young men and women who no doubt will be genetically programmed by us and therefore will be foolish enough to follow in our professional footsteps—what will they regret that we never did when we had the chance? When they read our books and essays, if indeed they bother to engage in such esoteric pursuits, what will they condemn us for not having had the foresight to investigate? Where and to what extent will we have hindered their own work? How will we have failed them?

I think these are important questions to ponder, for we are in the privileged position of being the first generation of African literature scholars. Twenty-five years ago hardly anyone was paid a salary to read, teach and interpret African literatures. Today a good many of us earn a relatively comfortable living explicating literary texts, most of which have been created during our own lifetime and some of which will certainly outlive us all. A majority of the authors of these texts are still among us, accessible to us in ways that future generations will envy. Even the few who are already gone still have a palpable residual existence in the hearts and minds of those who knew them personally as relatives, friends, enemies, colleagues, neighbors, confidants, and casual acquaintances. We are in the presence of a host of living witnesses to the birth, growth, and early maturation of written African literatures, some of them potent participant-observers in the creative act itself, others merely interested bystanders or, if academics, professional voyeurs.

I don't think we have yet made enough of the opportunities such proximity to living literary genius affords us. The books and articles we write tend to be text-bound, seldom venturing beyond the novel, play, poem, or essay we are scrutinizing, seldom striving to capture the essence of the unique individual behind the work. We are content to analyze the words and images on a page without reference to the peculiarities of the personality that produced them. We write as if the literary work has its own autonomous existence, a life entirely independent of its creator. We sometimes pride ourselves on our formalistic rigor, our attention to details and patterns that have no relevance to real life.

There are those who would defend the objectivity of such otherworldliness, insisting that the art and the artist are two separate concerns that need not be inextricably linked. Some would go further and argue that it is presumptuous of literary critics to base even their most oblique critiques on what they happen to have heard of the personal lives of those whose works they study. Why should what we say about a text be affected by what we know about its creator? Aren't we carrying biographical inquiry too far when we invade the privacy of perfect strangers?

These, I admit, are valid arguments, and I have no quarrel with critics who voice them and who persist in preferring to construct (or deconstruct) formalistic paradigms in an effort to achieve some measure of scholarly detachment. Such pursuits may not do the world much good, but they certainly cannot do it much harm either. In my view it's a matter of little ventured, little gained, but I don't begrudge anyone the right to fritter away his intelligence on engrossing trivialities. For this is the kind of indulgent fascination that anyone who is some distance from the source of a literary work can luxuriate in. It makes few demands on his historical understanding or on his ability to relate the work meaningfully to its social context or to its singular creator. It's the type of critical cop-out that traditionally has been the refuge of the expatriate or non-African critic, the foreigner who lacks direct immersion in an African literary culture and therefore can comment only in lucid abstraction on whatever intriguing word puzzles may claim his attention. This sort of bloodless criticism can be written anywhere, anytime, and by anybody.

The pity is that so many African scholars have been drawn toward empty, formalistic exercises when there is so much else that they, and they alone, are ideally situated to do to enrich African literary studies. Worse yet, it appears that no steps are being taken to ensure that the work they are shirking today can be satisfactorily completed by their successors tomorrow. The necessary groundwork is simply not being laid. We may be handicapping future scholars by ignoring their most basic requirements. And to cap it all off, we may be actively discouraging our students and ourselves from undertaking certain types of research that could lead to the discovery of tangible new knowledge. The grandchildren of our grandchildren will not thank us for this legacy of benign and benighted neglect of crucial fundamentals.

But before I get worked up and begin speaking in vacuous abstractions myself, allow me to pin all this down with a few pertinent examples. Ages ago—in 1972-73, to be exact—I spent much of a sabbatical year at the University of Ibadan library, which used to be a national depository library and therefore holds a good collection of early Nigerian periodicals. Just before I arrived, a handy list of these holdings had been published, and I started working methodically through them, trying to find out how much Nigerian literature in English had appeared in Nigerian media intended entirely for Nigerian audiences. It was purely a fishing expedition, and I didn't know what I might come up with. Every day I would put in my call slips at the librarian's desk, and some time later, ranging from a few minutes to a few hours depending on the availability and efficiency of student assistants, a pile of academic journals, popular magazines, and ephemeral newsletters would arrive at my desk. I became particularly interested in early university publications, especially those that emanated from students' groups at Ibadan in the late 1940s and early 1950s. These publications were festooned with names I could recognize, names of men and women who subsequently had made substantial reputations for themselves as writers. Here was evidence of some of their earliest published work, their first forays into cyclostyled print. My fishing expedition had landed a few whoppers—or rather, a few minnows spawned by slippery undergraduate smallfry who later had grown into very big fish indeed. I spent much of that year trolling for such small submerged treasures, and when I got back to Texas I spent the next several years writing up the results of my library adventures. Many of the chapters in my book *Early Nigerian Literature*, which attempts to deal with the emergence of an anglophone literary culture in Nigeria, were derived from the notes I took in those uncharted Ibadan waters.

In one of my essays it so happened that I ventured to examine the recovered juvenilia of an author who today is one of the truly great whales in the Nigerian literary lagoon, a creature so large and powerful and versatile that he nearly obscures outside recognition of all the smaller presences in the same pool. It has been rumored that this African Moby Dick has even come to the attention of the Swedish Academy, whose members annually award perhaps the fishiest of all literary trophies. Well, my exposure of the youthful exploits of this huge humpback apparently touched a raw nerve, for in a recent article of his own he publicly called me a nasty name, or what I take to have been meant as a nasty name: *hagiographer extraordinary*. This ironic praise-name has a nice resonance and rhythm to it, and I'm thinking of having it engraved on my tombstone, if only to win some points with real saints who might be inclined to intercede on my behalf in the hereafter. But it would be dishonest for me to do so, for the name obviously is a misnomer. Anyone who reads my essay will see that I do not canonize this writer. On the contrary, I take some pains to show that even the king of the deep employed some rather awkward strokes when first learning to swim. Maybe that was how I really gave offense. Perhaps I was not canonical enough in my remarks. Perhaps he actually meant to call me *hagiographer manqué extraordinary*—an equally euphonious epithet, no matter how barbarous it might be in French. Or could there have been some other imagined slight that triggered the errant name-calling?

What disturbs me far more than the name-calling itself is the prohibition that this writer wishes to place on biographically focused literary research. He bluntly warns African scholars to avoid sporting in such waters. Yet I would argue that it is precisely here, among retrievable documentary records—not just juvenilia but every published word by any author who deserves to be taken seriously—that important pioneering scholarly work can be done. In Nigerian literary studies, clearly it is Nigerian scholars who are best placed to do the deepest probing and make the fresh discoveries.

Juvenilia is only one small domain, and admittedly a minor one at best, in this unplumbed, invisible realm. Far more important would be a writer's letters. Are there any archives here or elsewhere in tropical Africa that are beginning to collect such vital documents? Where are Okigbo's letters? Where are Okot's? Where are those of Alex La Guma, Bloke Modisane, and Bessie Head, to mention only three of the latest South African casualties? Is anything being done now to preserve the literary remains of perished writers? If not, why not? Think of your grandchildren. Think of their grandchildren. Someday when one of them wants to write a literary biography of one of Africa's past literary giants, will he or she wonder where all the personal documents went and why no one of the author's own time and place, none of his kith and kin, no librarians or literary scholars, not even one of his lovers or drinking buddies, thought well enough of him to try to preserve some permanent record of his life for posterity? How is it possible to write a decent biography of an author without access to any of the unpublished documents he wrote?

Certainly there have been attempts to fabricate such footnote-free biographies in other times and other places. Shakespeare is a fine case in point. There are hardly any primary documents in his own hand that have been preserved—only a few signatures that are thought to be genuine. So biographical speculation has taken the place of biographical research, with each scholar, unconstrained by hard facts, floating free on the clouds of his own soft imaginings. Some glibly assert that Shakespeare didn't even write his own plays and poems, and today they back up these claims with massive computer print-outs and technical jargon. Schoenbaum's *Shakespeare's Lives* shows how such yarns, spun out again and again over nearly four centuries, have left a durable legendry but little concrete information about one of the world's most important writers. Do we want the lives of African authors to be subject to the same process of historical mutilation? This would be tantamount to collusion in grand Larsony, not petty Larsony, and in the eyes of our descendants we would be the bungling culprits who let the precious hard currency in the central bank of ideas get lost.

But let's return to real African examples, a good one this time, an example well worth emulating. Two years ago a black publishing house in Johannesburg, Skotaville Publishers, brought out a collection of Es'kia [Ezekiel] Mphahlele's letters entitled *Bury Me at the Marketplace: Selected Letters of Es'kia Mphahlele, 1943-1980*; the book was edited by N. Chabani Manganyi, a clinical psychologist who incidentally has also recently written a fine biography of Mphahlele based on these and other documents, including transcripts of tape-recorded interviews with "Zeke" and his acquaintances both in South Africa and overseas. This is probably the first collection of letters by an important African writer to be published since the eighteenth century, and it spans nearly four full decades of the author's life. The letters were published with Mphahlele's consent and collaboration, and they throw revealing light on his entire career. Read them and you will be convinced that this is exactly the type of intimate biographical record we need to understand not only Mphahlele the man but also the range of experiences and ideas that sparked his creative fires. The book can serve as a model of what can be achieved through systematic biographical record keeping, through documentary retrieval, through vigilant maintenance of a respect for facts. And please note that all this can be done, possibly with greater accuracy and efficiency, while an author is still alive. One only hopes that other writers nearing their golden years will follow Mphahlele's example and open up their lives for public scrutiny.

I am urging this because I believe that academic attention at some point inevitably turns from a great writer's texts to his thoughts and deeds—in other words, to the way he chose to live his life. The texts, of course, will continue to be the primary point of focus, but the life will come to occupy a significant place beside the canon, and for some scholars the life will assume even greater importance than the works themselves. Famous writers should simply face the fact that part of the price of literary immortality is an eternal public snoopiness about their personal behavior. Literary celebrities cannot wish away this invasion of privacy any more than movie stars or rock musicians can. Of course, they can try to contain it, and some may be tempted to influence, or even completely choreograph, the writing of their own life history by leaking false information of one sort or another. But the truth may out one day, and if it doesn't, there is always a possibility that the falsehoods might take on a life of their own and increase and multiply. A celebrated writer cannot expect to have his privacy and his celebrity too. Harry Truman used to say, "If you can't stand the heat, get the hell out of the kitchen!" To move completely out of the public eye, a writer could simply stop publishing his scribblings, and if he is lucky enough to have been a bad writer, he could perhaps take some satisfaction in knowing that people will have already forgotten the earlier sins he committed in print. But there aren't many writers who for the sake of anonymity would willingly abort their creative powers and choose silence in preference to communication. If there are such authors in this world, we haven't heard a great deal from them lately, and that is as it should be, for they couldn't have had much to tell us that would have been worth hearing anyway. Since making literature is by its very nature a social act, it is perverse for writers to behave unsociably and to deliberately withhold information from those who wish to understand them better. After all, it's the writer's own reputation, his own place in history, that is at stake.

There is one last category of retrievable documentation I would like to touch upon, one that has relevance for both biographical and textual studies. I am referring of course to literary manuscripts. If I approach this subject more gingerly than the others, some of you may know the reason why. As the proverb goes, "Once bitten, twice shy." Or, in its Nigerian variant, "Once beaten, twice shy." Since I have been both bitten and beaten on this issue, I am doubly shy about talking about it. But it is too important a matter to ignore entirely, so I must say a few words on the subject here and now.

Some of you will remember that back in 1978 I attended an African literature conference at Ibadan. I was on my way to Nairobi, but I was eager to stop by and join in the Ibadan proceedings because a few months earlier I had made what I regarded, and still regard today, as a major literary discovery: I had located, through fragmentary publishers' records, a full-length manuscript by Amos Tutuola that antedated *The Palm-Wine Drinkard* and had never been published. On the very same day, Maundy Thursday of Holy Week, Faber and Faber had discovered the long-lost manuscript of *The Palm-Wine Drinkard* in the dead files of a deceased editor who for many years had been Faber and Faber's liaison with Tutuola. The whole story behind these discoveries is too complex to relate here. Suffice it to say that I recognized in an instant the importance of both manuscripts and tried to arrange for the Humanities Research Center at The University of Texas at Austin to purchase both of them. This was not a furtive and unscrupulous act. I was hoping that Tutuola would be paid handsomely for them and that the manuscripts would thereafter repose in a university research collection where special pains are taken to conserve such fragile and delicate documents.

Well, I turned out to be wrong, dead wrong, regrettably on both counts. I am sorry to say that up till now in 1986, eight years later, Tutuola has not yet found a buyer for either manuscript and that both are not in any university research collection. Why not? I often ask myself that vexing question, and I'm not sure I know the correct answer. Perhaps some of you here today who observed certain transactions at Ibadan and Ife in the aftermath of the 1978 Ibadan conference can tell me what happened. All I know is what didn't happen, and no one has ever explained to me in any detail why there has been no follow-up in the eight intervening years. How long, good lord, how long!

Since I was one of the players in this mini-drama up to a point, let me at least recount what transpired during that brief hour I strutted and fretted on the Ibadan stage. As I said earlier, I was hoping to report to the conferees gathered there the discovery of the Tutuola manuscripts and the planned acquisition of both by the Humanities Research Center at The University of Texas at Austin. I was expecting to be applauded for these initiatives. Wrong, dead wrong, and again on both counts. How naive, good lord, how naive!

To put the whole thing in a kola shell, what happened was that some of my friends at Ife, upon getting wind of what was in the works, mounted a welcoming party, complete with national press coverage, and reminded me in a manner that captured my full attention that Nigeria's literary treasures belonged in Nigeria. Their tactics may have been a bit theatrical, but they certainly got their message across, and I am still grateful to them for having taught me this valuable lesson. I now totally agree with them, of course, and I have made no further efforts to persuade my university to acquire Nigerian manuscripts or any other African manuscripts for that matter. Such manuscripts belong in Africa. They must remain at home rather than migrate permanently abroad.

But before they can rest in peace, they need to be protected from going to pieces, and the best way to do this is to place them in the care of institutional libraries or archives equipped to deal with such documents. Is there any repository in Nigeria so equipped? If not, why not? Has any Nigerian institutional library or archive started collecting literary manuscripts? If not, why not? Are there no literature department chairmen, deans, or vice-chancellors in Nigeria who are prepared to devote a portion of the university funds they administer to the preservation of Nigeria's literary culture? If not, why not? Please forgive my monotonous aggressiveness. I'm only asking the questions that your posterity will ask of you.

You may wonder why I am so obsessed with the preservation of literary documents. The reason is that I believe that this way truth lies. I believe that future generations of scholars will be less cavalier than we have been in handling facts if we leave them reliable tools to work with. I believe that some literary truths are virtually impossible to establish in the absence of trustworthy records. And I believe we have an obligation not only to seek the truth ourselves but also to help others seek it. The future of African literary studies will be glorious only if we strive now to make it so.

When I started this talk, I said I would try not to offend anyone. At this point I realize I may have succeeded in offending everyone. However, my dance is now over, and I'm ready to sit back and kick off my boots. If your toes hurt, please forgive my innate clumsiness. I really didn't mean to be so rude among such good friends.

Works Cited

Achebe, Chinua. *Arrow of God*. London: Heinemann, 1964.

————. *Morning Yet on Creation Day: Essays*. London: Heinemann, 1975.

Anon. "Finding Their Voices." *Times Literary Supplement*, 16 September 1965, p. 791.

Auden, W.H. *Collected Poems*. Ed. Edward Mendelson. New York: Random House, 1976.

Bamgbose, Ayo. *The Novels of D.O. Fagunwa*. Benin City: Ethiope Publishing Corp., 1974.

Beier, Ulli. "D.O. Fagunwa: A Yoruba Novelist." *Black Orpheus*, no. 17 (1965), pp. 51-56.

Brutus, Dennis. *A Simple Lust*. London: Heinemann, 1973.

Fagunwa, D.O. "What the School Can Do." *The Nigerian Teacher*, 1, no. 4 (1965), pp. 46-48; no. 7 (1936), pp. 39-40.

————. "Writing a Novel." *Teachers' Monthly*, 6, no. 9 (1960), p. 12.

Gupta, Balarama G.S. "Chinua Achebe's *Things Fall Apart:* A Few First Responses." *Literary Endeavour*, 1, no. 2 (1979), pp. 55-61.

JanMohamed, Abdul. *Manichean Aesthetics: The Politics of Literature in Colonial Africa*. Amherst: University of Massachusetts Press, 1983.

Kothandaraman, Bala. "'Okoli's Death: A Pointer towards the Narrative Design of Chinua Achebe's *Things Fall Apart*' —Another View." *Journal of Literary Studies*, 4, no. 2 (1981), pp. 77-84.

Lindfors, Bernth. "Amos Tutuola and D.O. Fagunwa." *Journal of Commonwealth Literature*, no. 9 (1970), pp. 57-65.

————. *Black African Literature in English: A Guide to Information Sources*. Detroit: Gale, 1979.

————."Interview with Okot p'Bitek." *Mazungumzo: Interviews with East African Writers, Publishers, Editors and Scholars*. Athens, OH: Ohio University Center for International Studies, Africa Program, 1980. 134-49.

————. *Black African Literature in English: 1977-1981 Supplement*. New York: Africana Publishing Co., 1986.

————. *Black African Literature in English, 1982-1986*. London: Zell, 1989.

————. "The Famous Authors' Reputation Test." *Tensions between North and South: Studies in Modern Commonwealth Literature and Culture*. Ed. Edith Mettke. Würzburg: Königshausen & Neumann, 1990. 222-30. Revised and reprinted as "The Famous Authors' Reputation Test: An Update to 1986." *Semper Aliquid Novi: Littérature Comparée et Littératures d'Afrique: Mélanges offerts à Albert Gérard*. Ed. János Riesz and Alan Ricard. Tübingen: Narr, 1990. 131-43.

Mtshali, Oswald Joseph. *Sounds of a Cowhide Drum: Poems*. Johannesburg: Renoster Books, 1971.

Ngugi wa Thiong'o. *Homecoming: Esays on African and Caribbean Literature, Culture and Politics*. London: Heinemann, 1972.

Okara, Gabriel. "African Speech—English Words." *Transition*, no. 10 (1963), pp. 15-16.

————. *The Voice.* London: Deutsch, 1964.

Okot p'Bitek. *Africa's Cultural Revolution.* Nairobi: Macmillan Books for Africa, 1973.

————. "Literature Department Needs Overhaul." *Uganda Times*, 6 May 1982, p. 5.

Olubummo, A. "D.O. Fagunwa: A Yoruba Novelist." *Odu*, no. 9 (1963), pp. 26-30.

Pal, Dipak. "Okoli's Death: A Pointer towards the Narrative Design of Chinua Achebe's *Things Fall Apart.*" *Journal of Literary Studies*, 3, no. 1 (1980), pp. 29-38.

p'Chong, Lubwa. "A Biographical Sketch." *Artist the Ruler: Essays on Art, Culture and Values*, by Okot p'Bitek. Nairobi: Heinemann Kenya, 1986. 1-12.

Shakespeare, William. *The Tempest.* Ed. William Aldis Wright. London: Macmillan, 1893.

Wooldridge, Mike. "[Report from Uganda]." *BBC Arts and Africa*, no. 441G (1982), pp. 5-6.

INDEX

Index